CULTURAL ATLAS FOR YOUNG PEOPLE

THE MIDDLE AGES

MIKE CORBISHLEY

REVISED EDITION

Facts On File, Inc.

Cultural Atlas for Young People
THE MIDDLE AGES
Revised Edition

Published in North America by:
Facts On File, Inc.
132 West 31st Street
New York NY 10001

AN ANDROMEDA BOOK
The Brown Reference Group plc.
(incorporating Andromeda Oxford Limited)
8 Chapel Place
Rivington Street
London EC2A 3DQ
www.brownreference.com

Project Manager Kim Richardson
Editor Lionel Bender
Art Director Ben White
Designer Malcolm Smythe
Cartographic Manager Richard Watts
Cartographic Editor Tim Williams
Picture Manager Claire Turner
Picture Researcher Cathy Statsny
Production Director Clive Sparling
Editorial and Administrative Assistants Marian Dreier,
 Rita Demetriou
Proofreader Lucy Poddington

ISBN: 0-8160-5150-X

Set ISBN: 0-8160-5144-5

Facts On File books are available at special discounts
when purchased in bulk quantities for businesses,
associations, institutions or sales promotions. Please
call our Special Sales Department in New York at
(212) 967-8800 or (800) 322-8755.

You can find Facts On File on the World Wide Web at
http://www.factsonfile.com

Printed in China

10 9 8 7 6 5 4 3 2

Library of Congress Cataloging-in-Publication Data
available from Facts On File

Artwork and Picture Credits
All maps drawn by Lovell Johns, Oxford.
Artwork by Adam Hook.

Key: t = top, b = bottom, c = center, l = left, r = right

Title page Alan Hutchison Library. 5 Dominique
Martinez. 6–7 Malcolm Smythe. 10–11 Bridgeman Art
Library. 14l Richard and Adam Hook. 14r BM.
16 Equinox. 17 Scala, Florence. 18 KM. 18 BM.
19 Scala, Florence. 20t Service de Documentation, Paris.
20bl Equinox Picture Archive, Oxford. 20br Leonard von
Matt, Buochs. 21 Pierpont Morgan Library, NY.
22t Michael Holford. 22cl Norfolk Museums Service.
22–23 KM. 24 University Museum of National
Antiquities, Oslo. 25 Richard and Adam Hook.
27l Bodleian Library, Oxford. 27r British Library,
London. 28 English Heritage. 30 KM. 30–31 Michael
Holford, Loughton. 32 Richard and Adam Hook.
33t Bodleian Library, Oxford. 33b National Monument
Record. 34t A.F. Kersting, London. 34b KM.
36t Universitäts – Bibliothek, Jena. 36b KM. 38bl Sonia
Halliday, Weston Turville. 38br Master and Fellows of
Trinity College, Cambridge. 38–39 KM. 39t CF.
39bl CF. 39br Mike Corbishley. 40t Michel Vuillemin,
Troyes. 40b Robert Harding Picture Library Ltd.
41 Bodleian Library, Oxford. 42bl Dick Barnard,
Milverton. 42br KM. 42–43 Dick Barnard, Milverton.
44, 45 Sonia Halliday, Weston Turville. 46t Historik
Museum, Bergen. 46b Michael Dixon, Dover. 47t Master
and Fellows of Magdalene College, Cambridge.
47bl Kunsthistorisches Museum, Vienna. 47br
Christopher Page, Oxford. 48t Ronald Sheridan.
48b History of Science Museum, Oxford.
49tl Österreichische Nationalbibliothek, Vienna.
49tr British Library, London. 49bl Mary Evans Picture
Library, London. 49br Bibliothèque Nationale, Paris.

50–51 Bridgeman Art Library. 52t Michael Holford,
Loughton. 52b Victoria and Albert Museum, London.
52–53 Bibliothèque Nationale, Paris. 53t Graham Speake,
Oxford. 54t Bodleian Library, Oxford.
54b, 58 Bibliothèque Nationale, Paris. 58–59 KM.
60 Biblioteca Apostolica Vaticana. 62t Robert Harding
Associates, London. 62bl, 62br Michael Dixon, Dover.
63cr Leonard von Matt, Buochs. 63bl Michael Holford,
Loughton. 65l Franco Ragazzi, Bologna. 65r British
Library, London. 66t Edwin Smith, Saffron Walden.
66b Robert Harding Picture Library, London. 68t Alan
Hutchison Library, London. 68c Dick Barnard,
Milverton. 68b Zefa, London. 69 CF. 70t Biblioteca
Apostolica Vaticana. 70bl, br Bibliothèque Nationale,
Paris. 71 Musée Condé, Chantilly. 72 Michael Holford,
Loughton. 73 Sonia Halliday, Weston Turville.
74l University Library, Ghent. 74r Public Record Office,
London. 75 KM. 76tr Andrew Lawson, Oxford.
76cr Leonard von Matt, Buochs. 76bl Graham Speake,
Oxford. 77 John Fuller, Cambridge. 78t Zefa, London.
78c Dorian Gerhold, London. 78b Dr L. Beckel, Bad
Ischl, Austria. 80 Fairford, Glos. 80–81 KM. 81t,b Sonia
Halliday, Weston Turville. 82t Michael Dixon, Dover.
82b Ekdotike Athenon, S.A., Athens. 84bl Giraudon,
Paris. 84br Tretyakov Gallery, Moscow. 86–87 KM.
88, 90 Werner Forman Archive. 91 KM.

List of Abbreviations
BM British Museum. CF Chris Forsey. KM Kevin
Maddison.

Quote from *The Canterbury Tales* by Geoffrey Chaucer
taken from translation by Nevill Coghill (Penguin
Classics, Revised Edition 1977), Copyright 1951
by Nevill Coghill, copyright © Nevill Coghill, 1958,
1960, 1975, 1977.

CONTENTS

INTRODUCTION

THIS IS A BOOK ABOUT THE PEOPLES OF MEDIEVAL Europe. But what does the word "medieval" mean? It comes from two Latin words meaning "middle age." In fact many writers still call this period of history the Middle Ages, hence the title of our book. What were they in the middle of? The medieval age begins at the end of the Roman period in western Europe, about 350 CE. It ends with the discovery, by Europeans, of the world beyond Europe in the late 15th century.

We started by talking about "peoples" of medieval Europe. In this book you will read about a number of different peoples over a period that covers more than 1,000 years. Some of these peoples were relatively small in number but have had great influence on later periods. The Vikings were such a people. No huge armies of Vikings sailed from their homelands of Scandinavia but their influence can still be seen today in towns and settlements across northern Europe and beyond to Iceland, Greenland, and even North America.

Because there were a number of peoples looking for new lands or just eager for power, the boundaries between countries frequently changed. Here you will be able to read about, and follow on the maps, at least part of the story of each "country" in medieval Europe. Some of these became "world powers," as we say today. Part of the story of medieval Europe is the struggle between these world powers. For example, there were wars between Christians and the followers of the prophet Muhammad, whose religion is Islam — the Muslim peoples. You will probably already have read about the Crusades to win back the Holy Land (Palestine), but there were other struggles going on. There was also a conflict between different types of Christian worship.

How do we discover the evidence for the peoples of medieval Europe? As for all historic periods there are two main sources. Documents give us one form of evidence that can be read. Archeological evidence is the physical remains of the past — perhaps a leather shoe preserved in a well, or a great cathedral still in use today. These two very different types of evidence together help build up the picture we have of the past.

The book is divided into two main sections. The first, **A History of Medieval Europe**, looks at the development of the most important empires that set the boundaries in the past. The second section, **The Lands of Medieval Europe**, examines in greater detail the individual countries that we can all recognize today and their own histories.

The Middle Ages is an atlas so there are lots of maps to help you understand the development of Europe. As you read through the book, compare the various regions with the map of Europe today on pages 8 and 9 to see how different medieval Europe really was — the past is a foreign country! But there is much more to this book than just maps. In both sections you will find a number of special features that look at life in medieval times and at some of the remains that you can see today. Our story is arranged in double-page spreads, so you can read the book from beginning to end, or just dip into it to learn about a specific topic. The Glossary on page 92 contains definitions of historical terms used in the book.

Abbreviations used in this book
BCE = Before Common Era (also known as BC).
CE = Common Era (also known as AD). c. = circa
(about). in = inch. ft = foot. mi = mile.

Right The town of Cordes, in the Tarn region of France, founded in 1222.

TABLE OF DATES

	400	500	600	700	800
ARTS AND ARCHITECTURE		Christian Churches built in Rome, Jerusalem, Constantinople	532–37 St Sophia, Constantinople c. 550 Ravenna mosaics	c. 650 Sutton Hoo ship burial c. 698 Lindisfarne Gospels	735–804 Alcuin, scholar	c. 870 *Codex Aure* illustrated manuscri
CHRISTIAN CHURCH	313 Edict of Milan granting toleration to Christians	430 death of Augustine at Hippo Regius 451 Council of Chaceldon	526 death of St Benedict 560 Irish missions to Continent 590–604 Gregory I pope			817 Benedict of Ania reforms monasteries 860 Cyril and Method sent to Moravia
ROMAN EMPIRE	395 divison of the Empire		533 Africa restored to Roman Empire	610–41 Heraclius emperor	716–17 Muslim siege of Constantinople 717–41 Leo III emperor 730–843 iconoclasm	867–86 Basil I, first emperor of Macedonian dynasty
ISLAM				622 Muhammad goes to Medina 661–80 Muawiya, first Umayyad caliph at Damascus	762 foundation of Baghdad as Abbasid capital	909 foundation of Fatimid caliphate in N Africa
SPAIN		409 Vandals, Alans, and Suevi enter Spain	509 Visigoths defeated at Vouillé and fall back on Spain		711 Muslims invade Spain	c. 860 serious Viking assaults on Spain
FRANCE		486 Clovis defeats Syagrius	c. 507 conversion of Clovis to Catholicism	687 Pepin of Austrasia defeats Neustrians at Tertry	732 Charles Martel defeats Saracens at Poitiers 751 Pepin III becomes king of the Franks	888 Odo count of Par becomes king
ITALY		476 Odovacar king of Italy	536 Belisarius reconquers Rome 568 Lombard invasion of Italy	668 Constans II killed at Syracuse	774 Charlemagne becomes king of Italy	
GERMANY	341 Ulfila begins conversion of Goths 376 Goths cross the Danube	406 Germans cross the Rhine			772–804 Saxon wars	800 Charlemagne crowned emperor 843 Treaty of Verdun: empire divided
EASTERN EUROPE			Slavs begin to infiltrate Balkans			864 conversion of Bulgars
BRITAIN AND IRELAND			563 St Columba in Iona 597 Roman mission to England	664 Synod of Whitby	Mercian supremacy 731 Bede completes *Ecclesiastical History* 793 first Viking raids on England	836 Danes establishe at Dublin 899 death of Alfred Wessex king of England
SCANDINAVIA						860 Danes establishe in Iceland

Diocletian and Maximian, c. 300.

St Sophia, Constantinople, 532–37.

The emperor Charlemagne, crowned 800.

900	1000	1100	1200	1300	1400
c. 985 *Beowulf*	c. 1063 San Marco, Venice	1194–1220 Chartres Cathedral built	c. 1225–74 Aquinas 1265–1321 Dante 1266–1337 Giotto	1304–74 Petrarch 1345–1400 Chaucer 1377–1446 Brunelleschi 1386–1466 Donatello c. 1390–1441 van Eyck	c. 1400–74 Dufay 1452–1519 Leonardo da Vinci 1471–1528 Dürer

Viking ship, Oseberg, 10th century.

The Tower of London, c. 1080.

Sculptures from Chartres Cathedral, 1134–50.

The town hall, Siena, 1297–1376.

David by Donatello, 1430.

900	1000	1100	1200	1300	1400
911 foundation of Cluny	1046 Synod of Sutri – beginning of reform in Roman church	1115 foundation of Clairvaux 1179 Lateran Council III	1209 Franciscan order approved 1215 Paris university receives first statutes	c. 1309–77 Pope's residence at Avignon 1378 schism begins	1415–17 Council of Constance
963–69 Nicephorus Phocas emperor	1018 final defeat of Bulgars 1071 battle of Manzikert	1176 Manuel I defeated by Seljuksat Myriokephalon	1204 4th Crusade; capture of Constantinople 1261 restoration of empire		1453 capture of Constantinople
	1055 Seljuks capture Baghdad 1071 after Manzikert Seljuks occupy Asia Minor 1095 1st Crusade	1171 Saladin conquers Fatimid Egypt 1187 Saladin recaptures Jerusalem	1218–21 5th Crusade 1250–1517 Mamluk dynasty in Egypt 1291 last Latin states in Holy Land taken by Mamluks	1326 Ottomans take Bursa 1389 Ottomans defeat Serbs at Kosovo	1402 death of Timur the Lame 1453 Muslims capture Constantinople
929 Umayyad caliphate in Spain	1031 end of Cordoban caliphate 1085 Christians capture Toledo	1137 count of Barcelona becomes king of Aragon 1147 Lisbon captured from Muslims	1235–48 Catholics conquer Cordoba and Seville	1369 Trastamara dynasty in Castile	1479 Ferdinand V of Aragon marries Isabella of Castile 1492 discovery of "New World" 1498 Vasco da Gama reaches India
911 Rollo installed in Normandy 987 Hugh, first Capetian king of the Franks			1204 Philip II conquers lands in France 1210–29 Albigensian wars 1226–70 Louis IX 1284 war between England and France	1337 war begins between Philip VI of Valois and Edward III	1431 Joan of Arc burned 1477 death of Charles the Rash, last Valois duke of Burgundy
962 Otto I crowned emperor	1030 Normans established at Aversa	1130–54 Roger II king of Sicily	1212–50 Frederick II emperor and king of Sicily 1252 first florins struck in Florence	1347 plague reaches Genoa from Crimea 1385 Gian Galeazzo unites Visconti lands	1434 Cosimo de Medici returns to Florence 1454 Peace of Lodi
955 Otto I defeats Magyars at the Lech		1122 Concordat of Worms 1159–77 imperial–papal quarrel	1273 Rudolf of Hapsburg elected king of the Romans 1291 first Swiss alliance	1338 Declaration of Rense 1348 university founded at Prague	1419–36 Hussite wars
966 foundation of Poland 989 Vladimir of Kiev becomes Christian	1000 Otto III founds archdiocese at Gniezno 1001 kingdom of Hungary established		1241 Mongols defeat Christians at Legnica	1320 Polish kingdom reunited 1386 Poland ruled with Lithuania	1478 Ivan III takes Novgorod
973 first recorded coronation of an English king	1017 Canute becomes king of England 1066 Norman conquest of England 1086 Domesday Book	1154 Henry II first Angevin king of England	1215 Magna Carta 1284 English king establishes rule over Wales 1296 war with Scotland	1381 peasants' revolt	1483 Henry Tudor made king
995–c.1000 Olaf I king of Norway		1104 archbishopric of Lund founded		1397 Norway, Sweden, and Denmark united by Kalmar Union	

EUROPE

W HAT DO YOU UNDERSTAND BY THE word "Europe"? Perhaps it will depend where you live – whether your home is in Europe or in one of the other six continents, the great land masses that make up our world. For you, Europe might be a place you go to for a vacation or a place where you can see and wonder at the great monuments of the past.

EUROPE TODAY

One way to define Europe could be as the all the countries north of the Mediterranean and Black Seas, from Iceland and Portugal east to Turkey and the Russian border.

Another way could be as the European Union (EU). It has 15 member states which are: Austria, Belgium, Denmark, Finland, France, Germany, Greece, Ireland, Italy, Luxembourg, the Netherlands, Portugal, Spain, Sweden and the United Kingdom. A number of other states, including some former members of the Soviet Union, are poised to join it in the near future.

THE PHYSICAL SHAPE OF EUROPE

Yet another way of defining Europe is to look at the physical boundaries, especially those between the continents of Europe and Asia. These boundaries are the mountain ranges of the Caucasus (between the Black Sea and the Caspian Sea) and the Urals (in Russia), both just off our map to the east.

MEDIEVAL EUROPE

The definition of Europe we use in this book about the medieval period is quite different. It has to be. We must start with what the Romans thought of as their Empire – and add to it as necessary. We must add countries and areas at different times in the medieval period. To the question "What exactly is Europe?" a Roman would not have been able to give a reply. An educated person from medieval Europe would have known what the question meant and been able to respond.

Right This map shows you the modern boundaries of the Europe you are going to read about in this book. You will see that these boundaries are often quite different from those in the *medieval period. The physical features are important. Mountain ranges, seas, deserts, and rivers usually defined where people lived and where they could travel to.*

8

PART ONE

A HISTORY OF MEDIEVAL EUROPE

Above A 10th-century ivory bookcover showing Pope Gregory the Great at his writing desk.

Right Detail from an early medieval illuminated manuscript, the Lindisfarne Gospels. Lindisfarne Island, off the northeast coast of England, was a focal point of English Christianity from 635 CE to about 950 CE.

um secundum mattheu:

cnister

rod lice

eriu   ruot dur   pier   mid dr

EUROPE 350–1500 CE

Roman Empire
Diocletianic diocese boundary
East-west division of Empire, 395
Territorial boundary
● Important settlement

Scale 1 : 24 000 000
0   600 km
0   400 miles

North Sea
Baltic Sea
BRITAIN
●Londinium
ATLANTIC OCEAN
Colonia Agrippina
Rhine
Lutetia
GAUL
Loire
●Caesarodunum
Danube
PANNONIA
Burdigala
●Lugdunum
●Aquileia
VIENNENSIS
●Vienna
WEST ROMAN EMPIRE
●Ravenna
●Sirmium
Black Sea
SPAIN
Narbonne
ITALY
MOESIA
THRACE
Tagus
●Toletum
Corsica
●Rome
●Constantinople
●Emerita Augusta
●Thessalonica
●Ancyra
PONTUS
Sardinia
Balearic Is
●Amida
●Carthago Nova
Sicily
EAST ROMAN EMPIRE
●Smyrna
●Carthage
●Athens
ASIA
●Antioch
AFRICA
Cyprus
ORIENS
Mediterranean Sea
Crete
●Jerusalem

Left *Europe in 350. For centuries the Romans had increased the size of the lands they controlled. At its biggest there were probably as many as 60 million people living in the Roman Empire. It was always difficult to control parts of this great Empire, especially those provinces that were on the borders. The problem was ruling such a huge area.*

Diocletian (made Roman Emperor in 284) split the huge Empire into two. He ruled from the East and appointed Maximian to rule in the West. To help organize and control this Empire, he divided it into 12 dioceses — marked here on the map. After the Emperor Theodosius' death in 395 the Empire was ruled separately in East and West.

Frankish Empire
Frontier land (march)
East Roman Empire
Muslim land
Territorial boundary
Picts Name of people
● Important settlement

Scale 1 : 24 000 000
0   600 km
0   400 miles

Scots **Picts**
North Sea
Baltic Sea
NORTHUMBRIA
Danes
Welsh MERCIA
WESSEX ●London
ATLANTIC OCEAN
Cologne
Rhine
●Paris
●Metz
●Regensburg
Loire
Danube
FRANKISH EMPIRE
PANNONIA
●Poitiers
●Lyon
BULGAR KHANATE
●Venice
Slavs
●Oviedo
●Milan
●Belgrade
Black Sea
GALICIA
●Ravenna
SPANISH MARCH
Narbonne
PAPAL STATE
●Trebizond
Tagus
●Toledo
●Barcelona
Corsica
DUCHY OF BENEVENTO
●Durazzo
●Constantinople
●Lisbon
UMAYYAD EMIRATE
●Valencia
●Rome
●Thessalonica
●Ancyra
●Benevento
Sardinia
EAST ROMAN EMPIRE
Balearic Is
●Almería
Sicily
●Smyrna
●Tangier
●Athens
●Antioch
IDRISID CALIPHATE
AGHLABID EMIRATE
Mediterranean Sea
Cyprus
ABBASID CALIPHATE
Crete
●Jerusalem

Left *Europe in 800. By the year 800 the West Empire had broken down and several "barbarian" states had been founded. The Romans called those who lived beyond their boundaries, who did not speak their Latin language or live the Roman way of life, barbari — our word "barbarians."*

The East Roman (Byzantine) Empire based in Constantinople still kept its influence in the East, in southern Italy and Sardinia. Other parts of the old Empire in the West were ruled by the Franks and by the Muslims — followers of the religion of Islam — who dominated North Africa and the Mediterranean Sea.

The Frankish Empire under Charlemagne was Christian and tried to revive Roman traditions. But by Roman standards even the Franks were barbarians.

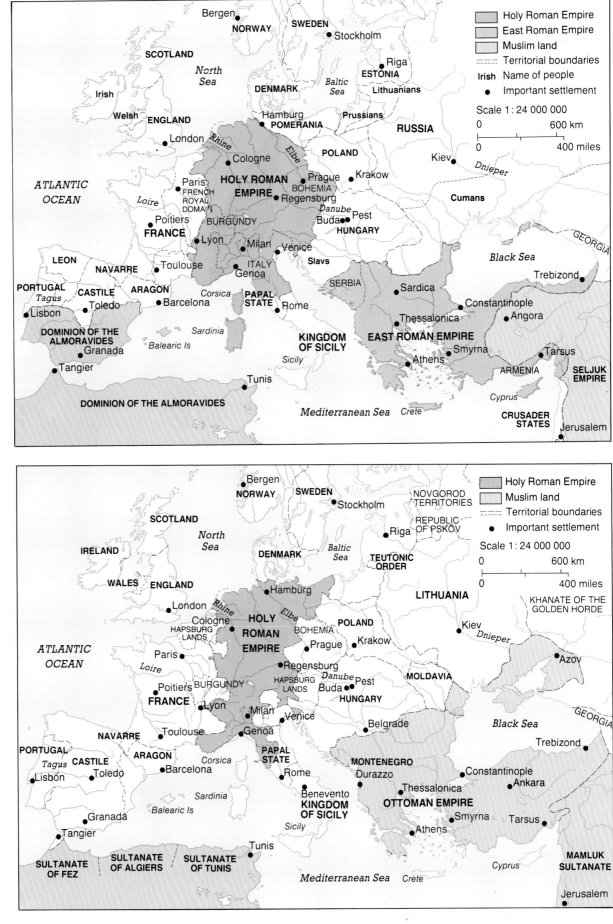

Right Europe in 1150.
By the 12th century Roman provinces that the Muslims had gained from the East Roman Empire were won back. Crusading Christians from the West had established Crusader states in the Holy Land, though they were under threat from the Muslims.

In the West, Christians had recovered parts of southern Spain and Italy. The Holy Roman (or German) Empire created by the Franks had strengthened its hold on Germany and Italy and had begun to expand eastwards into the territory of the Slavs.

At this time it looked as if a new Christian empire would expand to control as large an area as the Romans had once conquered.

Right Europe in 1500.
By 1500 great changes had occurred in Europe. Any hope that a Christian empire might be established throughout the Mediterranean was crushed by the success of a new empire — that of the Ottomans.

The East Roman Empire had been overrun by Ottoman Turks. Constantinople itself was captured in 1453. The eastern Empire could no longer be called Christian. The Holy Land, once protected by Western Christians, passed into the hands of the Muslims.

A different story was emerging in the West. Several smaller kingdoms were established and powerful rulers fought with each other for control of territories. Nations were being created, often out of a number of different peoples.

13

THE BARBARIAN MOVEMENTS

"The army of the Visigoths led by Athaulph marched on Gaul . . . The Romans were no longer able to win back Britain — from now on it continued to be ruled by whoever had seized power."

THE YEAR BEING DESCRIBED IS 411. THE writer is Procopius, a civil servant who was born about 500 and wrote, among other works, histories of the wars of the Roman Emperor Justinian. We have seen (page 12) that the Romans, in their vast Empire, had suffered from those peoples they called "barbarians." Not all these enemies were uneducated and murderous; they often wanted to rule their own countries and break away from Rome.

FROM THE NORTHWEST

From the countries to the north of the River Rhine tribes called Saxons, Angles, and Jutes invaded southern Britain. At first they settled alongside Romano-British communities in the eastern part of the country. Like many other barbarians, some were signed up as paid "mercenary" soldiers. Britain was unsettled, though, and many people fled to other parts of the country. Hoards of coins and valuables they hid have been discovered.

TERROR FROM THE EAST

"A report spread that the Goths had suddenly descended like a whirlwind from the high mountains and were ravaging and destroying everything in their path."

The historian Ammianus Marcellinus, writing in the 4th century, summed up the Romans' fear of the hordes of invaders. The Goths came from the steppes of Russia. There were two groups — Visigoths and Ostrogoths. Roman emperors paid some of them to stay out of Roman territory or persuaded some to move further west (to Italy and into Gaul). Despite this they were unstoppable, taking over huge areas that had once been Roman. Rome was itself plundered by the Visigoths in 410.

Below Unsettled conditions in eastern Britain meant that many people chose to bury their wealth for safekeeping. The scene below depicts the burial of the so-called Thetford treasure. This was a hoard of 4th-century gold and silver objects, probably buried by a merchant, from Thetford in Norfolk. It was discovered by chance in 1979 and is now in the British Museum, London.

Above This gold belt buckle, from the Thetford treasure, has a hinged bow in the form of two facing horses' heads. The high quality of the metalworking and the style of the figure suggest that it was made on the Continent in the late 4th century.

Above *Migrations of barbarians in the 4th and 5th centuries. There were many reasons for the movement of peoples from outside the Roman world and inside its boundaries. Some were looking for new farmland, but others enjoyed warfare.*

**Map labels:**

North Sea

Picts

Jutes
Angles

Angles
Saxons

Saxons

Angles
Saxons
London
Jutes

Franks

Rhine

ATLANTIC
OCEAN

WEST
ROMAN
EMPIRE
ARMORICA
Paris
Catalaunian
Plains
Orléans
Loire
Alamans
Worms
Danube
KINGDOM OF
ODOVACAR
Ostrogoths
Vandals, Suevi
Huns
Ostrogoths
Visigoths

Garonne
Burgundians
Lyon
Milan
Verona
Po
Drava
Gepids
WEST
ROMAN
EMPIRE
EAST ROMAN
EMPIRE
Plovdiv

Basques
Toulouse
WEST
ROMAN
EMPIRE
Ravenna

Suevi
VISIGOTHIC
KINGDOM
Ebro
Narbonne
Corsica

Tagus
Toledo
Barcelona

Sardinia
Balearic
Islands
Rome
Cosenza
Athens
Corinth
Sparta

Marsala
Sicily
Reggio

Carthage
VANDAL KINGDOM
Crete

Mediterranean Sea

Legend:

Barbarian movements
→ Franks
→ Huns
→ Ostrogoths
→ Saxons, Angles, Jutes
→ Vandals, Suevi
→ Visigoths

– – – Territorial boundary c.475
Angles Name of people
⚔ Major battle

Scale 1 : 16 000 000

0   400 km
0   300 miles

Saxons and others

By mid-5th century Saxons, Angles, and Jutes have begun to settle in Britain permanently.
410 In Italy, Rome taken by Visigoth chief Alaric.
493 Ravenna falls to Theodoric, king of the Ostrogoths. Theodoric dies fighting with the Romans against the Huns in 526.
West Roman Empire: 414 Visigoths take over Narbonne but abandon the town in 415.
436 Burgundians defeated by Huns at Worms.
451 Attila the Hun defeated by Roman general Aetius with help from barbarian troops at Catalaunian Plains. **486** Franks take over territory in West Roman Empire.
East Roman Empire: 382 Emperor Theodosius allows Visigoths to settle on the northern edge of the Empire. **468** Failure of Emperor Leo's expedition against Vandals.

BARBARIANS WERE HUMAN TOO . . .

Despite their reputation, the barbarians had their good side. It is true that they did not live a Roman way of life and hardly left any written record of themselves, but some, like the Goths, were Christians. Theodoric, King of the Ostrogoths, was Christian and well educated. In his capital, Ravenna in Italy, he built a number of important buildings, including churches, in the Roman style.

The Ostrogoths and other barbarians employed skilled metalworkers and jewelers to produce elaborate crowns, crosses, and bookcovers. They liked to wear jewelry on their clothes.

15

THE EMPIRE OF JUSTINIAN

THE ROMAN EMPIRE IN THE EAST continued to be ruled by emperors at the end the 5th century. But the situation in the West Empire was quite different. There, army commanders usually appointed emperors. In 476 Ordovacar, king of a group of German tribes who had settled in Italy, decided to rule instead of the Emperor Romulus Augustulus.

REOCCUPYING THE WEST

It was not until the reign of Justinian as Emperor in the East that the West Empire was brought under Roman control again. After he came to power in 527, Justinian's first move against the barbarians who had taken over the Empire was in North Africa. Vandals, originally from central Europe, had swept westwards, through Spain and into Africa early in the 5th century. Although the Vandals had set up a strong kingdom there,

Justinian's campaign won back North Africa in a few months in 533.

GENERALS BELISARIUS AND NARSES

The Emperor's two commanders attacked Italy from different directions. Belisarius occupied Sicily, Sardinia, and Corsica, and then moved into mainland Italy, finally reoccupying Rome in 536. After a century of fear, Rome was now freed from Vandal power in the Mediterranean.

Narses moved across land to lay siege to Ravenna in 540. Ravenna had become the official residence of the barbarian rulers of Italy – the Ostrogoth Theodoric, for example. There was some resistance to the reoccupation by Roman forces, but this was finally crushed in 552. Narses ruled the West, which now included a small part of Spain, from Ravenna as the Emperor Justinian's chosen governor.

Left This portrait of the Emperor Justinian is a small part of a large mosaic picture in the church of San Vitale, Ravenna, Italy. The building was begun by the king of the Ostrogoths, Theodoric, in about 520. Justinian had the church decorated with wall and ceiling mosaics in about 550.

Right The reconquests of Justinian. Compare this map of the countries around the Mediterranean with the one on the previous page. For a short period, at least, Roman authority was reestablished in the West by Justinian. Roman trade could now begin again across the Mediterranean.

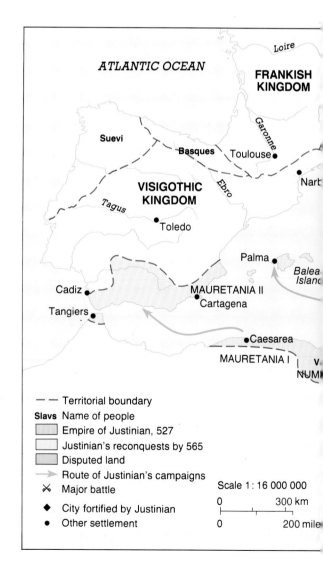

- - - Territorial boundary
Slavs Name of people
▨ Empire of Justinian, 527
☐ Justinian's reconquests by 565
▨ Disputed land
→ Route of Justinian's campaigns
✕ Major battle
◆ City fortified by Justinian
• Other settlement

Scale 1 : 16 000 000

0   300 km

0   200 mile

AFTER JUSTINIAN

Justinian died in 565. Italy was invaded by the Lombards in 568, but they were not able to take over the whole country. Only in the late 7th century were Africa and then Spain taken over by the Muslims. The East Roman Empire, also known as the Byzantine Empire, continued to be ruled by emperors until 1453 when its capital, Constantinople, fell to the Ottoman Turks.

Events of Justinian's reign

527 Justinian proclaimed Emperor with his wife Theodora.
533 Campaigns against barbarians in Africa and Italy.
535–54 Ostrogoths conquered in Italy.
552 Reoccupation of southern Spain.
Attacks from outside Empire: Slavs **534, 547, 549, 551**. Bulgars **534, 538**. Huns **539–40, 559**. Persian Emperor Khusrau I makes frequent attacks until peace treaty in **561**.
565 Emperor Justinian dies.

Above Part of the helmet of Agilulf, who was King of the Lombards 590–615. Even though the Lombards invaded Italy after Justinian's time, the decoration here shows Agilulf (center with the pointed beard) guarded by his warriors wearing Roman armor.

RAVENNA

Ravenna

RAVENNA, A PORT IN NORTHEASTERN ITALY, was enlarged in 23 CE by the first Roman Emperor, Augustus, who based his northern navy there. The city became much more important from 402 when it was chosen as the official residence of the Roman Emperors of the West so that they could have close links with the Emperors in the East in Constantinople.

IMPERIAL BUILDINGS

Buildings in Ravenna had to be splendid enough for the court of the Roman Emperor. One that survives today, and influenced later buildings, was the church of Sacra Croce (the Sacred Cross). It was built in about 425 by the Empress Galla Placidia, who was the mother of the Emperor Valentinian III.

Attached to the church was a mausoleum (a building for burial) with beautiful mosaics on its domed ceiling. They show a deep sparkling blue heaven with gold stars shining through.

CHRISTIAN CONQUERORS

In 493 Ravenna was captured by the Ostrogoth King Theodoric. He governed Italy from here with the help of Roman advisers. He had lived from the age of 8 to 18 in the imperial court at Constantinople. He was, therefore, a well-educated man. During his 30-year reign in Ravenna he put up a number of fine buildings and adapted or changed others. Many of these buildings were Christian churches.

REGAINED BY JUSTINIAN

The Roman Emperor in the East, Justinian, sent his forces to drive out the Goths from Italy. After Theodoric's death in 526 Ravenna remained an important city. Justinian had new buildings put up and others adapted – as he did elsewhere in the Empire.

In Ravenna the most important building was the church of San Vitale. The church was begun by the Ostrogothic Bishop of Ravenna but completed by Justinian. It was the official church of the imperial court, built of long thin bricks but with marble columns inside and decorated with splendid mosaics on its upper walls and domed ceilings. One mosaic is a picture of Justinian and Theodora bringing gifts to the holy altar.

Right This beautiful mosaic dome was commissioned by King Theodoric in Ravenna. It shows Christ being baptized in the River Jordan by John the Baptist (on Christ's left). If you follow around the dome you will see (above Christ's head) a cross on a cushion. You will need to look at the mosaic closely or with a magnifying glass to see the little pieces of stone that make up the picture.

Below Mosaics – pictures and patterns mainly in stone – were made by both Greek and Roman artists. Rich Romans, especially in southern Italy in places such as Pompeii, used Greek mosaic-makers to construct fine floor and wall pictures. The tradition continued in the East Roman Empire.

Tesserae

Three layers of mortar

Wall

Left Wall and ceiling mosaics needed a firm foundation. Three layers of mortar were applied. The cubes of stone, called tesserae, were often set at an angle to reflect the light.

Left Empress Theodora on a mosaic in the church of San Vitale. Her eyes are made of pieces of stone (above).

Above The mosaic-maker used mother-of-pearl for the Empress's headdress to make it look real.

CAROLINGIAN EUROPE

WHEN OSTROGOTHS RULED ITALY AND Visigoths ruled Spain in the 6th century, the countries we now know as France, Switzerland, Germany, Luxembourg, Belgium, and the Netherlands were ruled by a number of different Christian kings. The most powerful rulers were the Franks. They were right on the edge of the Christian world and fought against non-Christian peoples beyond (the Frisians and Saxons). They also established many monasteries in their lands.

The Frankish kingdom of Clovis was later divided into three parts: Austrasia, Neustria, and Burgundy. One of these kingdoms, Austrasia (now Germany), became powerful not only because its people were warlike but also because they controlled the main route between the newly established Christian communities in England and Rome itself. Pilgrims and monks had to go through Austrasia and across the Alps into Italy, as the route through southern Gaul (now France) was blocked by the Saracen Muslims.

THE CAROLINGIAN FAMILY

Charles Martel was the first of the Carolingian family to have a reputation in Europe – his name means Charles the Hammer. He defeated the Saracen Muslims at Poitiers (in western France) in 732. He made himself the most powerful ruler in the whole of Gaul. His son, Pepin III, won back lost territories and conquered new lands. He was the first of the family to become king of all the Franks.

By Pepin III's death in 768, the Frankish Empire stretched from the borders of Spain to the Netherlands, and east from the edge of Brittany to Bohemia.

CHARLES THE GREAT – CHARLEMAGNE

Pepin's two sons inherited his lands. When the younger son died in 771, the elder, Charles, became sole ruler. This Charles was called, in Latin, Carolus Magnus, or Charles the Great – Charlemagne. The word Carolingian comes from his name Carolus. Charlemagne reigned as emperor for over 45 years and increased the size of the Empire. He organized about 60 military campaigns – leading half of them himself. His wars against the Saxons were long, drawn-out, and brutal.

By the end of the 8th century the boundaries of the Carolingian Empire had moved north to take over the Saxon lands, south into Italy and east into Bavaria. The pope in Rome recognized Charlemagne's considerable authority and crowned him Emperor of the West. After Charlemagne's death in 814, his Empire continued to be governed by his only surviving son, Louis, at least for a time.

CHARLEMAGNE'S WORLD

Charlemagne had no capital city but in later years often ruled his huge Empire from his palace in Aachen, Germany. He was a ruler with a great interest in education and culture. Besides his own Frankish language he also spoke Latin. He understood Greek but never learned to write it.

Both in Charlemagne's time and during the reigns of later Carolingian kings, monks were encouraged to study manuscripts that had survived from the Roman and Greek worlds and to make new copies of them. It is because of this that we are now able to read the "classics."

Above A bronze statue of Charlemagne from Metz. Pope Leo III crowned him Emperor of the West on Christmas Day 800.

Right The back cover of the Lindau Gospels was decorated with gold, silver-gilt, and enamel in Charlemagne's time. The decoration of the intertwining animals is earlier.

Left and above Impressive religious buildings and objects show how important Christian worship was at this time. Left, the Carolingian church of a monastery at Corvey in northern Germany. Above, a 9th-century enamel cross, now in the Vatican.

SUTTON HOO

I N 1938 THE OWNER OF SOME LARGE BARROWS (mounds of earth) in Suffolk, England, wanted to find out what was inside. She asked the local museum to find her an excavator. The following year one of the most spectacular archeological discoveries of the century was made.

THE BURIAL OF A KING

Inside the largest barrow archeologists found the traces of a wooden boat 89ft long. Although the body had long since rotted away, it had been surrounded with many beautiful and priceless objects. The archeologists believed that this was the grave of an East Anglian king called Raedwald who died in about 625. Raedwald was also declared *Bretwalda* or High King of Britain, from about 616. Although the type of burial was pagan (not Christian), Raedwald was buried with some Christian objects. Possibly, he had been converted to the Christian religion.

Above The King's helmet has been reconstructed by specialists at the British Museum. It carries two emblems — a dragon over the crest and a bird across the face. The helmet and the sword and shield are similar to ones found in Sweden. Other objects show how far people traveled at the time — silver dishes from Constantinople were among the possessions of this English chief.

Above and right The King was laid out ready for his journey to the next world in a seagoing clinker-built ship. He had clothing (cloaks and leather shoes), spears and other weapons, and objects ranging from a lyre (a small harp) to a great bronze cauldron.

VIKING EXPANSION

"The ravaging of heathens destroyed God's church at Lindisfarne, with much plunder and slaughter."

THE VIKINGS (THE "HEATHENS" WRITTEN about above) were robbers who came by sea – pirates. This quotation is from the *Anglo-Saxon Chronicle*, a history of England put together in the 9th century. This entry is for 793. Many people had every reason to be frightened of these "wolves to be feared" as their warships sailed from their homelands in Scandinavia.

VIKINGS AT HOME

Vikings were actually several different peoples who lived in what we now know as Norway, Sweden, and Denmark. Many people think of them today just as warlike raiders. Not all Vikings were like that. They were farmers, great traders, and town builders. Their artists and craftspeople produced beautiful objects.

THE SEARCH FOR NEW LANDS

Many Vikings set off from their homelands in search of new lands to settle and farm, such as Iceland. Other voyages were carried out for plunder first, then for settlement. Norwegian Vikings began to settle in the islands off the north coast of Scotland at the beginning of the 8th century. From there they moved down the west coast of Britain and across to Ireland.

The Danish Vikings plundered Lindisfarne on the northeast coast of Britain and later East Anglia. Vikings from Sweden moved across the Baltic Sea into eastern Europe. Traveling by river, they eventually reached Constantinople, attacking it in 860.

By the 9th century Viking merchant-warriors had built up a large trading network across the Baltic Sea, linking Europe from end to end.

PLUNDER, SLAVES, AND TRADE

The Viking raiders certainly looked for and collected plunder but they also required slaves – they called them *thralls*. Some peoples they attacked were forced to buy them off with gold. Trade was important too. For example, a Viking prince established a trading contract by force with Constantinople in 907. The Vikings supplied slaves, timber, furs, and honey in exchange for gold, silver, and luxury goods. Before coins were used, the Vikings chopped up silver objects (often jewelry) and used them for exchange.

SHIPS AND THE SEA

The Vikings were great shipbuilders and sailors. This was the key to their success as traders, raiders, and settlers. They made very long voyages in fast ships, even crossing from Iceland to Greenland to settle in North America. Their ships, built with overlapping timber planks, were powered by sails and oars and had grand names such as "Sea-striding Bison" and "Long Serpent." The Vikings built not only "longships" for raiding (holding up to 200 warriors) but also wider trading ships called *knarrs* and little rowing boats called *faerings*.

Above Reconstruction of a ship excavated from a royal burial mound at Oseberg near Oslo in Norway.

Below Across the Atlantic. The search for new lands and an escape from murderous feuds took some Vikings far overseas. By about 1000 they had built settlements as far away as Labrador and Newfoundland.

Above A drawing of a Viking farmhouse at Stöng in Iceland, based on archeological excavations. Viking settlements here were destroyed by a volcanic eruption in 1104. The farm buildings were made of turf and consisted of hall, living room, dairy, and lavatory.

Below Viking settlements in Iceland and Greenland. Sheep farming was the basis of the Vikings' new northern settlements. Written records from these lands show the settlers as hardy and sometimes violent people, feuding and fighting. Some ventured even further west — to the North American coast.

Right Raids on Britain. Invasions of Vikings were difficult to stop. The Anglo-Saxon King Alfred halted them in 886 and reoccupied London. But a large area of Britain — known as the Danelaw — fell under Viking control. Not until the mid-10th century were they fully overcome.

Danish Viking settlement (Danelaw)
Norwegian Viking settlement
→ Viking raid
● Important settlement

Scale 1 : 7 500 000

0   150 km
0   100 miles

Shetland Is

Hebrides

Orkney Is

North Sea

SCOTLAND

Lindisfarne

NORTHUMBRIA
● Carlisle

BRITAIN

● Heversham

Isle of Man

● York

IRELAND
● Dublin

ENGLAND
● Lincoln
● Nottingham
Leicester ●
MERCIA
Worcester ●
Severn
● Pembroke
Thames

● Norwich
EAST ANGLIA

London ●

● Wexford

WESSEX
● Canterbury
● Winchester

To Normandy

English Channel

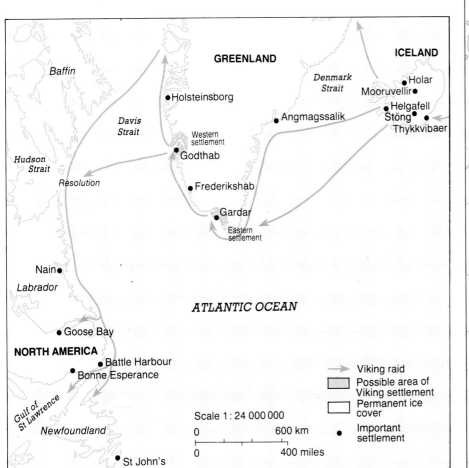

Baffin

GREENLAND

ICELAND

Denmark Strait

● Holar
Mooruvellir ●
● Helgafell
● Stöng
Thykkvibaer

Davis Strait

● Holsteinsborg

● Angmagssalik

Hudson Strait

Western settlement
● Godthab

Resolution

● Frederikshab

● Gardar
Eastern settlement

● Nain
Labrador

ATLANTIC OCEAN

● Goose Bay

NORTH AMERICA
● Battle Harbour
Bonne Esperance

Gulf of St Lawrence

Newfoundland

● St John's

→ Viking raid
Possible area of Viking settlement
Permanent ice cover
● Important settlement

Scale 1 : 24 000 000

0   600 km
0   400 miles

THE BYZANTINE EMPIRE

TODAY WE USE THE WORD BYZANTINE TO describe the East Roman Empire and Byzantium for the city of Constantinople. Constantine the Great, the Christian Emperor of Rome, made this ancient city (Byzantium) the capital of the East Roman Empire in 330. You have read earlier (page 16) how some parts of the West Roman Empire were lost to various barbarians, such as the Vandals, and how the Emperor Justinian later won back some territory.

THE THREAT FROM THE EAST

The greatest threat to the Byzantine Empire – the Holy Christian Empire – was from the Muslims in the East. Their religion was Islam, following their prophet Muhammad who lived in the 7th century, and they fought to establish their religion in other countries. By the 8th century they had occupied not only the Middle East but North Africa, Spain, and Portugal. The Byzantines held out against Islam, however. In the 9th century, under emperors from Macedonia in northern Greece, they began to push the Muslims back into Syria, and they later conquered the Bulgars in the north.

CONSTANTINOPLE

From the time of the first Macedonian emperors in 867, for about two centuries, Constantinople flourished. The Greek Orthodox Church began to send out missionaries to convert the unbelievers to Christianity. The Empire grew. Its capital city, Constantinople, also grew within the walls built by the Emperor Theodosius in the 5th century. The modern Turkish city there, called Istanbul, now fills the area laid out by Theodosius.

Constantinople was attacked many times in its history but the Byzantine Empire lasted until 1453 when the Ottoman Turks conquered the city.

Revival of the East Roman (Byzantine) Empire

May 11 330 Constantinople founded.
717–41 Reign of Emperor Leo III, who drives off Muslim attacks.
867 Beginning of reign of Basil I, first of the Macedonian emperors.
976–1025 Reign of Emperor Basil II, who conquers the Bulgars. Byzantine Empire at full extent by the end of his reign.
1176 Turkish Seljuks defeat the Byzantine Emperor Manuel I.
May 23 1453 Ottoman Turks take Constantinople. Byzantine Empire collapses.

Below The Byzantine Empire, showing its fullest extent by about 1025. The people known as the Bulgars were converted to the Orthodox Christian religion in 864, and their territory was conquered in 1018.

Right The Roman Emperor Justinian built the magnificent new church of Santa Sophia (it means Holy Wisdom) in Constantinople in 537. This is a view of it in 1852 by the architect Fossati, who was commissioned by the Turkish sultan to restore it. It had been converted to an Islamic mosque in 1453.

Above This little drawing of Constantinople, made in 1436, shows the great domed roof of the church of Santa Sophia and a statue of the Emperor Justinian on a horse.

THE PLANTAGENET EMPIRE

THE EMPIRE OF CHARLEMAGNE (PAGE 20) had stretched across the countries we now know as France, Italy, and western Germany. His Empire was eventually divided into three parts for his grandsons in 843. By this time there were also other divisions of territory created by powerful lords – dukes and counts – who had small armies to control their own lands.

SAXON ENGLAND

Since the Roman period England had been invaded and settled by different groups, first the Saxons, then the Danes. By the mid-11th century the king was Edward the Confessor, descended from Saxon and Norman families. On his death in 1066 there was no adult male in his family to succeed him. Harold Godwine, the Earl of Wessex and the King's brother-in-law, claimed the throne.

NORMANDY AND ENGLAND

However, William, Duke of Normandy, had other ideas. He invaded England in 1066, winning the Battle of Hastings and the throne of England.

From then the histories of France and England were linked together, and the English king played an important part in continental affairs. Over the next 140 years England and Normandy were usually ruled by one person, although at times the two countries were split between different kings.

THE PLANTAGENET FAMILY

The Angevin family, whose base was at Anjou in France, are called Plantagenets by historians. The name Plantagenet may have come from the sprig of a plant worn by Geoffrey of Anjou on his cap.

In December 1154 Henry II, the 21-year-old son of Matilda of England and Geoffrey of Anjou, came to England as king after the death of his cousin Stephen. Henry was already Duke of Normandy and of Aquitaine. He then led expeditions far into neighboring territories (building strong castles to impose his control) and increased the Plantagenet Empire. The lands he eventually controlled stretched from the borders of Scotland to the Pyrenees, but this "empire" was not to last.

Right The Plantagenet Empire. The Empire was bordered on the east by the lands of the king of France and on the south by various lordships. Henry II moved about his territory even when he was not fighting. He spent most of his time close to hunting reserves and frontiers – the Thames Valley, Southampton, Barfleur, and the Seine Valley.

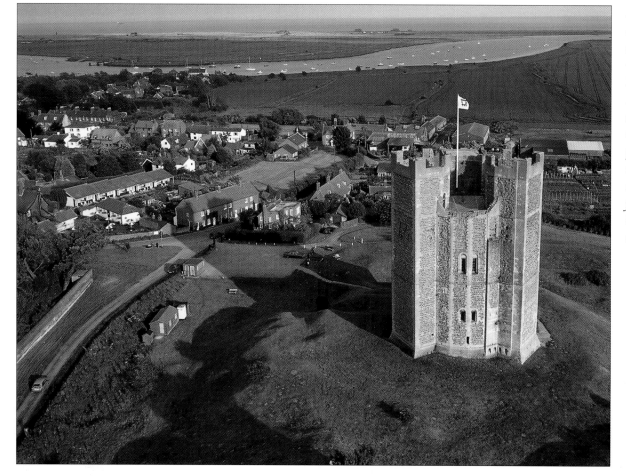

Left Henry II had a number of strong, stone castles built, especially along coasts which were open to attack. In England, Dover Castle was built by Henry II (although it has been added to over the years). So was Orford Castle in Suffolk, pictured here. Orford Castle took eight years to complete at a cost of more than £1400 – a fortune in the 12th century. The keep, the strongest part, and some earthworks still survive.

Linlithgow ▲
Edinburgh ▲
Berwick
Kelso ▲
Ayr ▲
▲**Roxburgh**

SCOTLAND

Dumfries ▲
Newcastle ▲
Carlisle ▲

North
Sea

Armagh ●
▲**Richmond**
Granard ▲
Lancaster ▲
●**Tuam**
▲**York**
Athlone ▲
Pontefract ▲
IRELAND
Dublin ●
●**Conisborough** ▲
Deganwy
Birr ▲
Beaumaris ▲ Rhuddlan ▲
Lincoln ●
Athy ▲
Trimahoe ▲
Caernarvon ▲ Conway ▲ ▲**Chester**
Limerick ●
Leighlin ▲
Hawarden ▲
ENGLAND
●**Cashel**
Ardfinnan ▲
▲**Shrewsbury**
Lismore ▲
Waterford ▲
WALES
▲**Leicester**
●**Norwich**
Aberystwyth ▲
●**Coventry**
●**Orford**
▲**Builth**
●**Colchester**
Cardigan ▲
Hereford ●
●**London** ▲
Pembroke ▲
Llandaff ●
Thames
▲**Canterbury**
●**Wells**
●**Salisbury**
▲**Dover**
●**Winchester**
Southampton ● ●**Chichester**
●**Hastings**
Exeter ●

ATLANTIC

OCEAN

English Channel

●**Barfleur**
Seine
●**Rouen**
●**Bayeux**
▲**Château Gaillard**
NORMANDY
●**Evreux**
St Pol de Léon ●
●**St Malo**
●**Avranches**
●**St Brieuc**
MAINE
FRANCE
BRITTANY
●**Rennes**
●**Le Mans**
●**Vannes**
▲**Tours**
Nantes ●
Loire
▲**Chinon**
●**Bourges**
ANJOU
Loudun ▲
POITOU
TOURAINE
Mirbeau ▲
●**Poitiers**
LA MARCHE
●**Saintes**
Clermont-Ferrand ●
Bay of Biscay
AUVERGNE
Périgueux ●
AQUITAINE
VELAY
●**Bordeaux**
●**Mende**
Garonne
●**Cahors**
●**Uzès**
Agen ●
QUERCY
●**Albi**
●**Lodève**
GASCONY
●**Aire**
TOULOUSE
Bayonne ●
●**Auch**
●**Toulouse**
●**Béziers**
●**Maguelone**
Lescar ●
●**Narbonne**
●**Oloron**
●**Comminges**
NAVARRE
FOIX
Mediterranean
Sea
PYRENEES
ARAGON

— Boundary of Plantagenet
Empire, 1154

Ruled by Stephen until 1154

Ruled by Henry II from 1149

Acquired by Henry II, 1151

Acquired by Henry II, 1152

Acquired by Henry II,
1154–1189

Disputed land

- - - Boundary of Plantagenet
Empire in France, 1226

Toulouse, 1154

▲ Castle
● Other settlement

Scale 1 : 5 000 000

0   150 km

0   100 miles

Plantagenet power

In France: Henry II becomes Duke of Normandy in
1149, Count of Anjou in 1151, and Duke of
Aquitaine in 1152.

England in 1154: Stephen is King of England until his
death in 1154 (Duke of Normandy 1135–44). Henry
II becomes King.

Campaigns:
1157, 1163, 1165 Wales.
1159 Toulouse. 1166 Britanny.

New territories acquired: 1159 Quercy.
1171 Britanny (by the marriage of Henry II's son,
Geoffrey).
1171 Henry is recognized as lord in Ireland and in
Scotland in 1174 but never rules there.

THE BAYEUX TAPESTRY

THE FAMOUS BAYEUX TAPESTRY IS AN exciting account in pictures and in words of the events that led to the successful Norman invasion of England in 1066.

It begins: "EDWARD REX. UBI HAROLD DUX ANGLORUM ET SUI MILITES EQUITANT AD BOSHAM." This text, in Latin, provides the caption for the picture-story. It means "Edward the King. Where Harold, Duke of the English, and his soldiers ride to Bosham."

HAROLD AND WILLIAM

When Edward, King of England, died in 1066 there were two powerful leaders who claimed the throne – Harold, the English duke, and William, Duke of Normandy. At the beginning of the tapestry we learn that Harold traveled to Normandy and swore to support William. But as soon as Edward died Harold claimed the English throne. William prepared for invasion and war in England. He built a great fleet and on September 28 sailed to Pevensey in Sussex on the south coast of England. The Normans landed their army, horses, and supplies and then built a timber-and-earth castle at Hastings. Meanwhile Harold hurried south after defeating King Harald of Norway near York.

Below The Bayeux Tapestry is not really a tapestry, because it was not woven. The pictures and words are embroidered in colored wools on linen. It is over 230ft long and 20in wide. William's *half-brother, Bishop Odo of Bayeux, probably ordered it to be made. The work was probably completed in England and then taken to France to be displayed at Bayeux Cathedral.*

THE BATTLE OF HASTINGS

William had an army of about 7,000, including 2,000 cavalrymen. The English army was smaller but fought well at a place later called Battle. The tapestry gives all the gory detail of the battle; arrows and spears fly through the air and men are cut down. Finally Harold is wounded and killed. The English have a Norman king – William the Conqueror.

REDISCOVERING THE TAPESTRY

Although the tapestry remained safe in the cathedral at Bayeux, it was not discovered to be an important historical "document" until the 18th century. It was moved several times during the Second World War, but it is now on display to the public in a special building.

Left *The tapestry is a marvelous source of illustrations of the 11th century. It shows a number of buildings, such as churches, castles, and towers. William's invasion fleet has ships built in the Viking style (long and clinker-built).*

Below *The battle scenes show us how men fought at the time and the weapons and armor they carried — conical helmets with nose protectors, chain mail, shields, swords, and axes. Here King Harold is wounded with a Norman arrow and then cut down.*

DOMESDAY BOOK

THERE ARE MANY DIFFERENT KINDS OF written evidence for the medieval period. They include histories, surveys, laws, court hearings, wills, and inventories (lists) of property in houses. Some of these documents have survived and can be studied today.

KING WILLIAM'S SURVEY

The Bayeux Tapestry provides evidence for William the Conqueror's invasion of England. Another important document has survived to help us understand what the conquered land of England was like – this time a written record.

In 1086 King William ordered a survey of all his English lands to check that he was receiving all the

Right King William, "after much thought and very deep discussion with his council," so the Anglo-Saxon Chronicle says, sent commissioners throughout England to collect the information for the Domesday Book. In each village or town a jury had to answer questions about the people and the resources of their lands. Other information collected included the number of clergy and churches.

Terra Epi Herefordenfis. In Writa. ten& Epc. ii. hid. 7. xx. ac. qru una fuit in eccla t. r. e. 7 alia feudo haroldi. Sep. iii. uilt. 7. i. pbr. Tc. ii. bor. m. viii. Tc. ii. fer m null. sep. i. car in dnio. 7. ii. car hom. filu. c. porc. viii. ac. pti. Val. l. fol.

XIX.

TERRE Comitis Euftachij In Exffeffa. Hund de berdeftapla. **.XX.**
Phobinge tenuit Brictmar un teinn regis Eaduuardi p. v. hid. 7. p uno man. m ten& comes. E. in dnio. Sep. iiii. car in dnio. 7. v. carruc. hominu. Tc. viii. uilt m. iii. Tc. viii. bor. m. xxii. Tc. xii. fer. m. vi. Silu. dcc. porc. Paft. dcc. ouib;. dim pifcina. xxxi. porc. dcc. ou. 7 xvii. Ex hac tra tulit Turold. xxx. ac. quæ st ad feudu epi baiocenfis. Pt hoc addidit Ingelric huic manerio. xxii. libos hoes tenentes. xv. hid. 7. dimid. 7. xv. ac. 7. dim. In q tra. st sep. xii. car. 7. xx. bord. 7. iii. fer. Silu. l. porc. x. ac. pti. Paft. cccc. ou. Tcia pars uni pifcinæ. 7 poft addi. iiii. car. 7. dim. Tc ual. maneriu. xx. lib. 7 tra. fochemanoz. xii. lib. M int totu. xxxvi. lib.
Horninduna ten& Garner de comite qd tenuit Vluric lib ho. p. uno manerio. 7. p. ii. hid. 7. l. ac. Sep. ii. car. in dnio. Tc. ii. uilt. m null. Tc. vii.

Translation of the Domesday Book entry (boxed area):
Brictmer, a thane of King Edward's, held FOBBING for 5 hides, as one manor. Now Count Eustace holds it in lordship.
Always 4 plows in lordship; 5 men's plows.
Then 8 villagers, now 3; then 8 smallholders, now 22; then 12 slaves, now 6.
Woodland, 700 pigs; pasture, 700 sheep; 1/2 fishery. 31 pigs, 717 sheep.

rents and taxes to which he was entitled. This survey came to be known as the Domesday Book and was referred to for many years afterwards. In fact, there are two volumes of records. The Great Domesday surveys most of England, while the Little Domesday covers only the counties of Essex, Norfolk, and Suffolk. Not every place was recorded – the towns of Winchester and London, and large parts of the north of England, were left out. Today the Domesday volumes are kept in the Public Record Office in London.

WHAT IS RECORDED?

King William wanted a record of who owned the land at the time of his invasion of England in 1066 and who held the land 20 years later, in 1086. The Domesday Book records this as *then* (before 1066) and *now* (in 1086). It states that William gave land to friends, such as Odo, the Bishop of Bayeux, who fought with him at Hastings. It also records the number of plow teams a village had. Most of the population were "villeins" and "bordars," who were villagers who held varying amounts of land in the estate or village. "Slaves" were owned by the lord and had no land for themselves.

The Domesday Book also gives some information about animals and the amount of land available for feeding and pasturing animals. If the village had other resources, such as fishponds, mills, beehives, and salt-works, they too were recorded.

Above The entry in the Domesday Book for the village of Fobbing in Essex tells us that Brictmer was lord of the manor under the Saxon king Edward the Confessor. King William gave Fobbing to Eustace, Count of Boulogne, who fought at the Battle of Hastings. The entry shows that in 1066 there were eight villeins (tenants), in 1086 only three, and so on. The entry finishes with a list of other resources.

Left An aerial photograph of Onley, Northamptonshire, a village in medieval times, now deserted except for a modern farm on the site. What you can see are the earthworks — the only remains of fields, gardens, houses, and streets. The most striking feature is the way the fields were plowed in strips leaving furrows on each side.

Around the barn (top center) is the village itself with "hollow ways," or deeply cut tracks, running through it. On each side are the individual plots of land for the villagers.

THE CRUSADES

IN THE AREAS OF EUROPE THAT HAD BECOME Christian – Christendom is the general name often used – there were many devout followers of the religion. Religious "orders" were set up, and followers lived in religious communities of monks and nuns. Special religious objects (such as the bones of a saint) and holy places (shrines) were treated with great respect. From the 4th century, within the Roman Empire people made special journeys called pilgrimages to these holy places.

The Holy Land of Palestine was the most important destination for pilgrims. But the shrines of St Peter and St Paul in Rome became popular among pilgrims, especially after Jerusalem was taken by the Muslims in 638.

THE HOLY LAND – LOST TO CHRISTIANS

The Arab Muslims, followers of the prophet Muhammad, did not stop Christians from visiting the Holy Land. However, in 1076 Turkish Muslims captured Jerusalem from the Arabs. They turned Christians away, arresting and torturing some pilgrims. The Christian emperor in Constantinople called for help in fighting these Turks.

FIGHTING FOR CHRIST

To help the emperor, Pope Urban II in 1095 called for a "crusade" ("war of the cross") to win back the Holy Land from the "unbelievers." Huge numbers joined the cause and "took up the cross." The First Crusade won back Jerusalem within four years, killing the inhabitants and establishing a kingdom there. Other crusades followed. There were many problems – not only in fighting the enemy but between the "Latin" Christians, who were led by Rome, and the "Greek" or "Orthodox" Christians, whose capital was Constantinople.

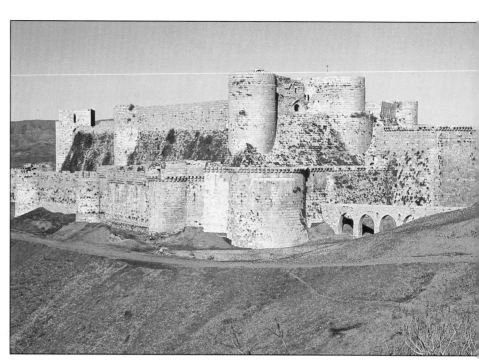

Above Krak des Chevaliers in Syria, a huge castle built by crusaders. Crusading knights formed into different "orders." Krak was held by the Knights of St John the Hospitalers (they were dedicated to defending the sick) from 1142 to 1271.

The Crusades: success and failure

First Crusade 1095: 1095 Crusade called for in the West by Pope Urban II. 1096 Crusaders reach Constantinople. 1098 Antioch besieged and captured. 1099 Jerusalem captured.
Second Crusade 1145: 1145 Edessa lost. Crusade achieves nothing.
Third Crusade 1189: 1174 Saladin, Sultan of Egypt, captures Damascus, 1183 Aleppo, 1187 Jerusalem. 1189 Crusade led by Emperor Frederick of Germany, King Richard I ("Lionheart") of England and King Philip II of France. Coastal towns and forts recaptured.
Children's Crusade 1212: Several thousand children go on crusade. Those who reach Alexandria are sold as slaves.
Crusade of 1248: Led by Louis IX of France, who is captured by the Egyptians and ransomed.

Right Crusader states. The crusaders set about founding states in the Holy Land that could be held against the "unbelievers" and be organized like those in western Europe.

Left A crusading army led by knights on horseback besieges a Muslim castle. Footsoldiers fought with spears and crossbows, and large siege-engines were also used. These included mangonels, which hurled great stones at the walls and could kill as many as 12 men with their blows.

▲ Castle
◆ Fortified city
● Other settlement

Places under the control of
● Knights Templar
● Teutonic Knights
● Knights of St John the Hospitallers

COUNTY OF EDESSA 1098–1145
PRINCIPALITY OF ANTIOCH 1098–1268
COUNTY OF TRIPOLI 1109–1289
KINGDOM OF JERUSALEM 1099–1187

Crusader states
After 1st Crusade

Scale 1: 12 500 000

Saladin's conquests
Before 3rd Crusade

Scale 1: 12 500 000

Scale 1: 2 000 000
0   60 km
0   40 miles

THE GERMAN EMPIRE

THE WEST ROMAN EMPIRE HAD A LONG AND complicated history. Previous maps show how it emerged from earlier empires to become the most important state in Europe. From 962 it was called the Holy Roman Empire. Earlier in this period it is sometimes called the Saxon Empire, as it was ruled by Saxon kings. The rulers of the Empire were all Germans.

KING HENRY OF GERMANY

The lands of Germany were divided into duchies, lands belonging to dukes. Each duke was powerful and had his own army and castles. They did recognize kings but often fought against them. In 919 Henry, Duke of Saxony, succeeded the previous king, Conrad of Franconia. At first Henry had authority over only these two areas but he was eventually recognized as Henry I throughout Germany.

ENEMIES ON THE BORDERS

The Germans had two main enemies – the Magyars (Hungarians) and the Slavs. Henry I tricked the Magyars into a truce while he built castles and fortress towns, such as Quedlinburg and Merseburg. In the war of 933 he beat these enemies. The Slavs were more difficult as they had settled in large numbers and were farming lands north of the River Elbe. Gradually, though, the German kings extended their territory eastwards.

OTTO I – EMPEROR

Henry's son Otto came to the throne in 936. He made the German dukes his subjects. One writer at the time said that the dukes "gave him their lands and promised him their loyalty and help against all enemies." Otto attacked the Magyars and finally defeated them in 955. He extended his authority in other ways too. In 951 he became King of Italy and he was crowned Holy Roman Emperor in 962.

THE HOLY ROMAN EMPIRE

Otto saw himself as the natural successor to the Emperor Charlemagne. His title was Imperator Augustus – Emperor Augustus. To maintain his authority, Otto installed his own cousin as the pope Gregory VI in 996. In 998 his grandson Otto III proclaimed that the old Roman Empire was now revived. The people of Rome itself, however, never really liked these German emperors and rose up against him.

Left Scenes from the life of Pope Gregory VII (1073–85), from the Bishop of Freising's World Chronicle. The Emperor Henry IV of Germany campaigned in Italy against the Pope. These four scenes describe the dispute, showing more sympathy for Gregory (top center and right) than for Henry (top left). They also give an early example of how history could be tellingly depicted by pictures from this period.

Map labels

North Sea

German Empire
— — — Boundary, c.962
— — Regional boundary, c.962
Duchy
Associated state
March
—— Boundary, 1158
Slavs Name of people
◆ Fortress town
● Other settlement

Scale 1: 6 500 000
0   100 km
0   75 miles

Oldenburg
Lübeck
MARCH OF THE BILLUNGS
Slavs
FRIESLAND
Bremen
Havelberg
NORTH MARCH
Minden
Hildesheim
Magdeburg
Oder
Münster
SAXONY
Paderborn
Quedlinburg
MARCH OF LAUSITZ
Utrecht
Merseburg
MARCH OF MEISSEN
Antwerp
Meissen
LOWER LORRAINE
Rhine
Cologne
THURINGIA
Liège
MARCH OF ZEITZ
Cambrai
FRANCONIA
Mainz
Prague
KINGDOM OF BOHEMIA
Trier
Main
Würzburg
Olomouc
Moselle
GERMAN EMPIRE
Vltava
Metz
Nuremburg
UPPER LORRAINE
Speyer
Regensburg
Toul
MARCH OF AUSTRIA
Strasbourg
Danube
BAVARIA
Passau
Vienna
KINGDOM OF FRANCE
Augsburg
Magyars
Rhine
SWABIA
Salzburg
Basle
L Constance
Seckau
Besançon
Constance
Inn
Mur
KINGDOM OF HUNGARY
Chur
CARINTHIA
L Geneva
Brixen
Geneva
VERONA
KINGDOM OF BURGUNDY
Aquileia
Trieste
Vienne
Lombards
Verona
Venice
Po
Milan
Mantua
Turin
Piacenza
KINGDOM OF CROATIA
Viviers
Embrun
KINGDOM OF ITALY
Genoa
Ravenna
Arles
PAPAL STATE
Adriatic Sea
Pisa
Mediterranean Sea

Left Drawing from a manuscript of 1425 showing a panmaker at work in Nuremburg, Germany. The panmaker is using a pointed hammer to pierce the bowl-shaped metal utensil repeatedly to produce a colander for straining. A medieval kitchen would contain all the cooking utensils we know today.

Above The German Empire (Holy Roman Empire). The main boundaries show how the Empire grew. The kingdoms of Italy and Burgundy were absorbed in the 10th and 11th centuries, but the Lombards of northern Italy were always troublesome. Noble families and princes became increasingly powerful in Germany itself.

A March was a frontier territory often disputed with the neighboring kingdom or country. It was heavily militarized at all times. A Duchy was a territory controlled by a duke (or duchess) and with its own laws. Associated states were, at various times, ruled by their own kings.

German expansion

919–36 Henry I is King of Germany. Campaigns against the Slavs and Magyars.
955 Otto I finally defeats the Magyars.
967–70 Attempts to gain territory in southern Italy.
1033 Kingdom of Burgundy added to Empire.
1158 Kingdom of Bohemia added to Empire.
1158 March of Lausitz, **1163** Duchy of Silesia, Opol, and Ratibor, and **1181** Duchy of Pomerania under German control.
1194 Kingdom of Sicily acquired by Henry VI.
1231 Teutonic Knights win Prussia.

THE MEDIEVAL CHURCH

THE CHRISTIAN CHURCH DEVELOPED slowly at first in the Roman world. By the 3rd century Christianity was spreading quickly. Bishops were in charge of Christian worship in communities all over the Roman Empire. Being a Christian was not always easy in the Roman world, but after 312 Christians were not persecuted for their religion. Christianity finally became the "official" religion of the Roman Empire in 395 under the Emperor Theodosius.

CHRISTIAN MONKS

The word "monk" comes from a Greek word for alone – *monos*. The first Christian monks lived alone, away from other communities, in the Egyptian desert. The first religious communities of nuns were also established in Egypt. Monks and nuns did not marry and lived apart from all comforts and luxuries.

The idea of the monastic life spread through the Roman world – not only in the eastern Mediterranean but also in North Africa, Italy, Gaul (France), Britain, and beyond the Roman provinces in Ireland.

MEDIEVAL MONASTERIES

After the Roman period many monasteries were founded that followed the Rule (or code) of St Benedict. Other "orders" of monks and nuns were also established. For example, a community was established in 909 at Cluny in Burgundy. By the next century there were 1,450 Cluniac communities throughout western Europe. Monasteries were important places of pilgrimage and learning.

THE ORGANIZATION OF CHRISTIANITY

The system of organizing Christianity for the community was set up in the Roman period. Bishops were appointed to areas called dioceses. Priests or vicars served individual communities in parishes within dioceses. A church was built for each community, but its size and structure depended upon what each parish could afford.

The shape and architecture of the parish church varied enormously across the Christian world. In theory all Western religious communities looked to Rome and the pope as the central authority. Often, though, communities acted as they thought best.

Above An illustrated letter B from a Bible now in Winchester, England. The Bible was made for the Bishop of Winchester, Henry of Blois, in the late 12th century. Part of the picture shows Jesus driving out devils.

Right This 12th-century illustration shows a monk making a copy of the Bible. These beautifully illustrated handmade books were highly treasured, and only a few survive today from the early periods.

Above and right The church at Wroxeter in Shropshire, England, stands in one corner of a Roman town, most of which is now hidden under grass fields. There may have been a Christian community here in the Roman period.

In the 9th century a decorated Anglo-Saxon cross must have stood in the churchyard (above), Parts of this cross survive in the wall of the aisle of the church. Crosses were centers for worship.

Most parish churches in Britain have a long history (right). There may have been a church here even before the one built in the 7th or 8th century. The Anglo-Saxon builders used large stones from the Roman town to construct their nave and chancel. The Domesday Book (pages 32–33) records four priests here in 1086.

Tower

Aisle

Chancel

Nave

Chapel

Porch

800–900

1200

1300

1400

Above and right The church at Wroxeter today has additions from many centuries. Now the entrance is through the 19th-century porch. Porches in the medieval period were often used to conduct parish business.

The aisle allowed more people to be in the congregation at services, and there was often a chapel in the aisle (as here) built by a wealthy person as a place for the priest to pray for the soul.

The nave was where the congregation stood (there were usually no seats in a medieval church). The chancel was where the priest conducted the service. The tower had the bells to summon the people to the service.

This view of Wroxeter Church (right) shows the Anglo-Saxon nave and the tower.

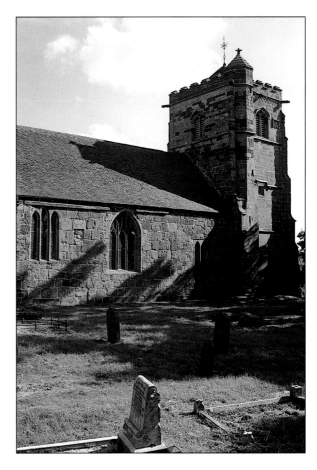

EDUCATION

IN THE MEDIEVAL PERIOD, FOR MOST PEOPLE education or learning, either reading or writing, served no practical purpose. There were many people – both workers and the wealthy – who could not read or write. But the clergy in the churches did need to be educated.

LITERATURE FROM EARLIER PERIODS

Manuscripts from the Romans (and a few Greek ones) survived long enough for monks to copy them out and to study them. Not all those involved in religion were educated. But clergy who served country parishes needed skills in reading, writing, and music, as few children were able to attend schools.

SCHOOLS

Schools were established for children, either as part of monasteries or by the bishop. For example, Lanfranc, appointed Archbishop of Canterbury, England, in 1070, set up a school at Canterbury for local children. Parish priests also did some teaching. The 12th-century historian Ordericus Vitalis was sent to a priest in Shrewsbury, England, at the age of five and

Left Nicholas of Lyra, seen teaching here in the center, was a monk from Normandy who taught at the University of Paris in the 14th century. Like most other teachers he gave lectures to his students in a very formal way.

learned reading, grammar, and music before taking holy orders to become a monk.

UNIVERSITIES

Places where students could continue their studies longer were being established by the church from the 12th century onwards, in particular for priests and monks to attend. The most famous universities were at Paris (for philosophy and religion), Bologna in northern Italy (for law) and Salerno in southern Italy (for medicine). In England, the first colleges were established in Oxford and Cambridge in the 13th century.

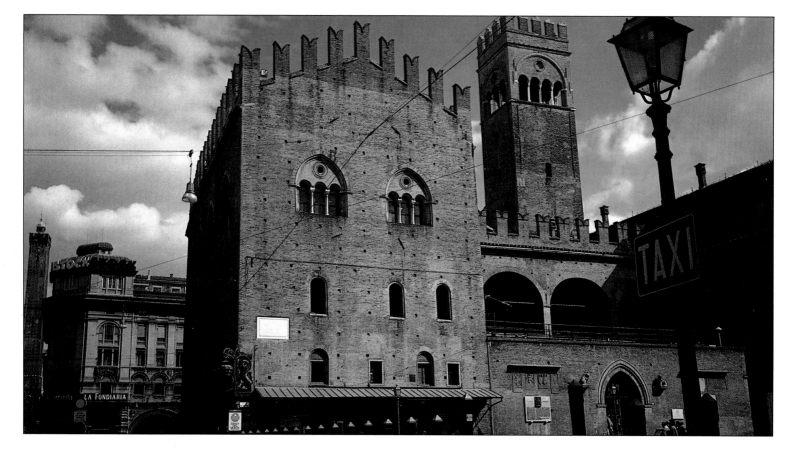

Right Hugh of St Victor teaching in his monastery at St Victor in Paris. Hugh became the prior, or leader, of the college in 1133. This was a college of canons who followed the Rule of St Augustine. A canon was a clerk who lived according to a Rule (the word in Greek for "rule" is kanon). The illustration here is from one of Hugh's own works in a manuscript edition made in the 13th century. This copy is now in the Bodleian Library of Oxford University, England.

Left The medieval university of Bologna, northern Italy, was grouped in two areas, close to each other, inside the walls of the city. The famous law school was in the center. The building you can see here, in the center of the medieval university area, is the Palazzo of King Enzo built in 1246 and used as his prison for 23 years until his death in 1272. The university grew very quickly during these years.

CATHEDRAL-BUILDING

WE KNOW THAT CATHEDRALS ARE usually large, grand churches, but the word itself can be traced back to the Romans. In Latin *cathedra* means professor's or teacher's chair. The word was used in the medieval period in exactly the same way – both Hugh and Nicholas are illustrated seated at their cathedral on pages 40–41. The word for "seat" becomes "important church" because a cathedral was where the seat or throne of the bishop of the diocese was.

SIZE AND SHAPE

Cathedrals are usually large, but it is possible to find some ordinary parish churches in England, for example, which are larger than cathedrals. A cathedral was also either secular (served by canons who were clerks) or monastic (served by monks).

A secular cathedral building would stand on its own like a big church. A monastic cathedral would be a church building attached to a whole group of other buildings for the monks to live and work in. There would be, for example, a chapter house (for daily meetings, announcements and sometimes punishments), a refectory (dining room), an infirmary (hospital), kitchens, a dormitory (large room for sleeping), a lavatorium (for washing), and a reredorter (lavatory).

A NEW STYLE OF BUILDING

In the middle of the 12th century in France a completely new style of church-building was developed. The Gothic style with its elaborate architecture and glass-filled windows allowed the building dedicated to God to be filled with "the new light," as one writer put it.

These buildings were very expensive and often took many years to complete. Gervase, a monk at the cathedral church at Canterbury, England, wrote in 1174:

"The master-mason, William of Sens, began to prepare all that was necessary for the new building and to destroy what was there before. This took the first year. In the next year he put up four pillars and after the winter two more . . ."

A master-mason might work with about 30 experienced craftsmen who traveled from job to job. Masons cut their own special mark in each stone they carved so that they could be paid for this "piecework," Local people would be brought in for the unskilled jobs, such as carrying stone.

COLUMNS, AISLES, AND ARCHES

This new style of architecture involved new types of building techniques, which the planners and masons (stonecutters) had to invent and test. The techniques did not always work – occasionally buildings fell down.

Cathedrals needed to hold large congregations of people but they had to look as if they were worthy to be called "houses for God." The builders of Gothic architecture were the first to discover how to put up very tall buildings of stone without enormously thick walls to carry all that weight. This discovery allowed them to design and build churches that looked beautiful both inside and out.

Below Cathedral-building involved lifting enormous blocks of stone. Two types of crane are shown here – the winch (left) and the treadwheel (right).

Right It took a lot of skill to be a mason, cutting and carving stone accurately.

Left This cutaway drawing shows that the inside of the cathedral is made bigger by aisles of columns on each side. Compare the building's size with that of the people on the ground.

Below The extraordinary height of Gothic cathedrals is possible because of these "flying buttresses," which help carry the weight of the building outside on columns and arches.

Below Part of the strength of these buildings was in their vaulted arches. They were constructed of stone over a wooden frame that was taken away when the stone construction was finished.

Right In France the new Chartres Cathedral was rebuilt after a fire in 1194. The money for this large Gothic building came from four trade fairs held each year on feast days of the Virgin Mary. A special feature of cathedrals from the 12th century is the huge rose window of stained glass.

STORIES IN STAINED GLASS

"The church shines, with its middle part brightened."

THE "NEW LIGHT" DESCRIBED BY ABBOT Suger, the leader of a community of monks in the early 12th century, was brought about in churches and cathedrals by the lightness of the building, towering to the sky, and by the light that streamed in through the windows. Not just white light came in – the light was made all the colors of the rainbow by stained glass.

CREATING AN ATMOSPHERE

Churches and cathedrals were built to honor God. Those responsible for the building may have wanted to show how wealthy and powerful they were, but it was even more important to create the right atmosphere for those who came to worship. Gothic buildings, as we have seen, were very impressive buildings – it is almost impossible not to wonder at them.

The atmosphere inside the church was created by sculpture, paintings, and the elaborate ceremonies full of chanting and music. Perhaps even more important was the "feel" created by the stained glass all around. Like the glittering effect of Byzantine mosaics, stained glass helped the worshipers to feel they really were in a special place.

STORIES IN THE WINDOW

Many people could not read so they were unable to discover for themselves the stories in the Bible or to learn from them, as their priests wanted them to. Stained glass, and also wall paintings, allowed them to "read" the stories for themselves. In many cases, however, it would be difficult to get more than just an impression of the story in windows high up in cathedrals. The story of Christ's life, and especially his death, was a favorite subject. The saints (there were a great number of them in the medieval world) and their lives were often pictured.

MAKING A WINDOW

It is easy to appreciate from the pictures shown here that making stained-glass windows was a skilled job. Glass was made from a mixture of ash from the wood of beech trees and washed sand heated to a very high temperature. The color produced was greenish and it was difficult to see through. To produce bright colors different kinds of metal, such as iron and copper oxides, were added to the mixture.

The glass was cut into small pieces and joined together to make up the picture with little strips of lead. Lines of paint were also added to produce a picture in glass. Sections of these leaded pictures were held together with iron rods and fitted into the carved stone window frames.

Glass painters, like masons, traveled from place to place for work which they were commissioned to complete.

CHARTRES

One of the best buildings in which to see stained glass is Chartres Cathedral in northern France. After a disastrous fire in 1194, the cathedral had to be rebuilt. Most of the medieval windows which were constructed and painted by craftspeople still survive today.

Above This rose window is in the church of Notre Dame (Our Lady) in Paris. It was made by two craftsmen in about 1270. The shape of the window and the colors used allow light to sparkle through into the church.

Right A 12th-century window at Chartres Cathedral. Between 1200 and 1235 more than 100 stained-glass windows were made. This work was paid for by a variety of people – from King Louis IX to the Count of Brittany and from the rich merchants in the city to the masons who worked on the building.

The scenes here are from Christ's last days – for example, the Last Supper and washing the feet of his disciples (bottom).

Right A chapel window in Strasbourg Cathedral, in France, made in the mid-14th century. Later windows such as this were made using the technique of painting on larger sheets of glass. The scenes here show the Resurrection of Christ.

MEDIEVAL ARTS AND CRAFTS

ONE OF THE MOST EXTRAORDINARY aspects of the medieval period in Europe is the range of works of art created by skilled craftspeople. Decoration was everywhere, from the complicated fronts of cathedrals to the metal clasps on Bibles. All sorts of techniques were used, such as carving in stone and wood, metalwork, painting, stained glass, and tapestry making.

BUILDERS IN STONE . . .

You have seen before how stonemasons were used to create cathedrals to be wondered at. Sculptors provided decoration for both the inside and outside of these buildings – on windows, columns, and towers. Doorways especially were often highly decorated with intricate carvings of birds, horses, and leaves. Medieval cathedrals also had a great number of carvings of individual people in niches (indentations in walls), especially about people from the Bible, saints, popes, and kings.

. . . AND IN WOOD

Wood does not survive as well as stone, but there are still a great many examples of the medieval woodworker's craft. Wood was very important in building, especially up to the 12th century. Even after that most ordinary buildings were of wood. Skills were developed to create complex constructions in wood. A manuscript describes the new wooden tower of Ely Cathedral, England, in 1328 as

"the ingenious wooden structure, designed with great and astonishing subtlety . . . huge beams cut and cunningly made into frames for the work by clever craftsmen."

WRITERS

We have already seen some examples of literature from the medieval period. Historians have left us information about people and events in the past. There were also many poems and stories. The clergy wrote mainly in Latin, but gradually the languages that people spoke were used for literature too.

Stories that retold tales from the classical (Greek and Roman) periods were very popular. So was heroic poetry, usually recited aloud, praising the skills and exploits of warriors. Here is a short translated extract from *Beowulf*, a poem written in

Left Early surviving examples of wood carving, such as this small figure of the Virgin Mary from the church at Griske, Sunnøre, Norway, show that craftsmen of the period had already acquired great expressive power.

Right A pattern book made in about 1380 showing various birds (the bullfinch is labeled). Pattern books were used by designers, wood carvers, and people doing embroidery.

Below The wooden roof of a small parish church in Garway, Herefordshire, England, shows the skill of local carpenters. The roof frames have beams that tie the outside walls together (tie beams), collar beams to hold the frame together, and braces.

Old English in the 8th century about a Germanic hero who overcomes monsters but is finally slain by a dragon:

> *"Then the dragon awoke, anger was renewed; he stalked along the rocks, with brave heart he had found the fiend's footprints; he had stepped with stealthy craft, near the dragon's head."*

MUSIC

Music was very important in medieval life. A special way of singing psalms (chanting) in monasteries was developed and became part of monks' daily services. Plainchants were sung in monasteries from the earliest periods. After the 11th century other lines of melody were added. Outside of religious life, traveling performers known as troubadours recited poetry and tales and sang accompanied by instruments such as trumpets, bagpipes, and lutes.

Below left Pope Gregory the Great at his writing desk with his symbol, the dove. He was pope in the 6th century. This beautiful 10th-century carving is made of ivory (animal tusk) and was the cover of a book now in a museum in Vienna, Austria.

Below This illustration is from a medieval Spanish manuscript and shows two musicians. The manuscript also has some lines of music drawn out (not shown here) to help singers accompany the players.

SCIENCE, MEDICINE, AND PRINTING

THE MODERN WORD "SCIENCE" COMES from the Latin word *scientia* meaning "a knowledge of." Classical and medieval people wanted a knowledge of a great many things that they saw around them but did not always understand. Knowledge and inventions from the Greeks and Romans passed to the Eastern Roman Empire in Constantinople.

MUSLIM TECHNOLOGY

Muslims in the East acquired this knowledge and developed it, collecting as much information as they could. For example, an 11th-century author, al-Bakri, says that the caliph (ruler) ordered a full survey to be made of the Roman aqueducts (for providing a regular water supply) in northern Tunisia so that ideas could be gained to develop their own system. The Muslims were skillful observers and recorders, and invented accurate measuring instruments.

PASSING ON THE KNOWLEDGE

The Christian medieval world often came into contact with Muslims and their knowledge in the 12th century, particularly in Spain and Sicily. Scholars began to go to these countries to learn from, and to translate, the manuscripts they found there.

A number of inventions were very practical, such as the magnetic needle in the compass for navigation, or spectacles to discover the science of light. Many ideas were outlined — some ahead of their time, such as the helicopter drawn by Leonardo da Vinci as early as 1486.

MEDICINE

The science of medicine and healing was well advanced in classical times. In the medieval period, though, herbs were the main source of treatment. Some remedies that doctors used then we do not use today. For example, the medieval treatment of bleeding with a leech (a blood-sucking water worm) probably stopped many people getting better.

Medieval people also believed in God's direct power over their bodies — the Plague was thought to be punishment from God. Their belief in the "influence" of the atmosphere around them to cause sickness gives us the name *influenza*. Folklore, the beliefs passed from generation to generation, played a major part in medicine and healing.

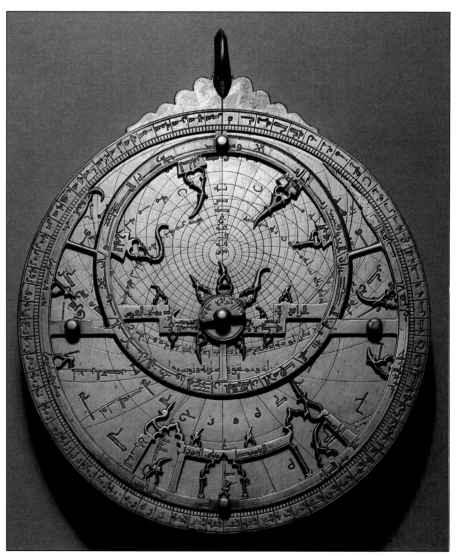

Left Model of a gear and barrel-like spring system invented by Leonardo da Vinci, 1452–1519, the great Italian painter, sculptor, architect, engineer, and scientist.

Right Page from a book on medicine written by a doctor in Baghdad in the 11th century. The text explains how marrows can be used for thirst and to clean out the bowels.

Below Astrolabes are for observing the sun and the moon and making accurate measurements. The astrolabe shown here was made by a Muslim in Spain in 1068.

Above Two of the 96 illustrations which were included in a textbook for doctors written by Roger of Salerno (in Italy) in about 1170. Here a doctor, dressed in the long gown of his profession, examines patients suffering from ailments in the leg and knee.

HOW PRINTING DEVELOPED

Passing on knowledge was difficult in the medieval world. There were schools and universities, and there were books as well, but these had to be laboriously copied out by hand. There was no quick and easy way of reproducing ideas and information.

By the 14th century paper not only had been invented but was in good supply. Religious pictures, some with lettering added, could be produced by means of wood blocks (using the same method as a linocut or potato print today). Engraving was also used for illustrating books. Maps were printed from engravings in several German towns and in Venice.

THE FIRST PRINTED BOOK

The next stage was to make individual letters of metal that could be put together to make up a page of text. The inventor seems to have been Johann Gutenberg in the town of Mainz in Germany. The earliest printed book was probably Gutenberg's *Book of Psalms* of 1457.

The idea was spread by German printers to Paris, Venice, and Rome, and by 1500 there were 250 towns in Europe that had their own printing presses. Venice was an important center, with 150 presses at work there. Knowledge and new ideas soon spread via books throughout Europe in a variety of languages.

Above A printing press in about 1520. The press pushes the inked block on to individual sheets of paper.

Right Two playing cards printed in about 1470. Printing was not always for serious purposes.

PART TWO

THE LANDS
OF
MEDIEVAL
EUROPE

Scandinavia
pages 88–89

Poland, Lithuania
and Russia
pages 84–85

British Isles
pages 66–67

France
pages 54–55

Germany, Switzerland
and the Low Countries
pages 78–79

Spain and
Portugal
pages 72–73

Italy
pages
60–61

Bohemia, Hungary,
Greece and the Balkans
pages 82–83

Above *Key to maps in this section of the book.*

Right *A 14th-century illustration depicting a scene from* Roman de la Rose, *a medieval love poem by two French writers, de Lorris and de Meung.*

TRAVEL

"Whan that Aprill with his shoures soote/
The droghte of Marche hath perced to the
roote . . . Thanne longen folk to goon
pilgrimages."

*"When in April the sweet showers fall and pierce the
drought of March to the root . . . then people long to go on
pilgrimages."*

THIS IS THE OPENING OF A LONG POEM
called *The Canterbury Tales* by Geoffrey
Chaucer written in the late 14th century.
The poem is about a group of people who join
together to make the five-day journey from London
to Canterbury to worship at the shrine of St
Thomas à Becket.

During the medieval period all sorts of people
made long journeys, though travel was not nearly as
easy as it is today or even as it was in the Roman
period. Traveling musicians and actors entertained
pilgrims, and others, on the road and in the inns.

ROADS

During the hundreds of years of the Roman
Empire a huge network of roads had been
developed. It allowed the army to move swiftly
from one trouble spot to another. It also allowed
merchants to trade across countries, and news and
ideas to spread. You can still see Roman roads
today, and so they were certainly used by people in
the medieval period. There was no imperial highway
authority to maintain the roads (as there is today),
though local sections and bridges were looked after
and improved. Tolls (travel taxes) were paid on
some roads.

The Canterbury pilgrims did not choose to
travel far, but many pilgrims did. They undertook
dangerous journeys right across Europe to Rome
and on to the Holy Land, or to the shrine of St
James the Great in Compostela in northern Spain.

STAYING THE NIGHT

Travel was not easy, comfortable or safe. There were
few places where travelers could put up for the
night. Monasteries had a duty to accommodate
travelers, and if you were rich enough you could
stay at manor houses or castles on the way. Others
had to make do at inns, which were not obviously
dangerous. Most people traveled on horseback,
although an elaborate cart, called a char, with a
canvas roof was available in Chaucer's time.

Above Here the Bayeux
Tapestry shows one of William
the Conqueror's specially built
ships for his invasion army of
1066. In shape it is very
similar to Viking boats. It has no
oars but is driven by sail, with
a steering rudder at the stern
(back).

Below Travelers in the early
16th century in Holland arrive
for May Day celebrations on
horseback, on foot, and by boat.
The river boat is paddled easily
by one person, while the
musicians play, and the man on
the prow fends off the arches of
the bridge.

Right A medieval bridge at
Karitaina in southern Greece,
built by the Franks in 1254
near their castle. Notice the
small chapel with a cross on top
half-way across.

Below This 15th-century
illustration from The Book of
Marvels shows travelers from
Europe outside the walls of
Beijing (China). The artist did
not know what it looked like and
so had to make up the view.

MOVING GOODS

Merchants often had to move their goods over long distances. Wherever possible, water transport was used, as it had been since prehistoric times. It was cheaper and easier than road transport. Crusaders saw very different types of ships in the Mediterranean from those used in northern Europe.

Finding the way was much improved by medieval inventions – the compass and the astrolabe. The astrolabe was still used until the 18th century. Other maps, as we shall see on pages 74–75, were in use from the 14th and 15th centuries.

FRANCE

OST IMPORTANT CHANGES IN THE government of France took place in the 13th century under King Louis IX. He became king in 1226 and reigned until his death in 1270. If you look again at the map of the Plantagenet Empire (page 29) you will see the differences which had taken place. The map here shows the later situation in France and Belgium in the 13th century. The dukes of Burgundy ruled the large territory that included the land still known as Burgundy today, though it never became a state.

THE REIGN OF LOUIS IX (ST LOUIS)

Under previous kings of France the lands ruled directly by the king had been extended. Under Louis IX the kingdom did not grow. He wanted to put a stop to the violent way disputes were being settled and encourage people to use the law courts. The *parlement* was the main royal court of law. Some of the new territories were ruled by Louis' brothers; others were under the King of England's control. For six years Louis fought a crusade against the Muslims. He was once captured and had to be ransomed.

At home, during his reign, he encouraged education and the church. The first French universities were founded. In Paris there were many artists, masons, and sculptors employed on new works. Paris became the most important center of book production of the time.

Left This illustration from a 15th-century French manuscript shows the assassination of John the Fearless, Duke of Burgundy, in 1419 at Montereau.

Above Before machines were invented, farmers had to use flails to beat the seed from cornstalks. Here a 15th-century French book shows this happening at harvest in August.

Feet
6500
4875
1300
650
0

Important settlement

Features located at a settlement
Monastery
Castle
University
Boundary, 13th century

English Channel

Bruges
Ghent
St Omer
Tournai
Arras
Schelde
Somme
Arques
Corbie
Fécamp
Premontré
Aisne
Rethel
Rouen
Beauvais
Reims
Caen
Seine
Pierrefonds
Château Gaillard
St Clair
Royaumont
Coutances
Marne
Châlons
St Evroult
Paris
Seine
St Pol de Léon
Montfort
Mt St Michel
Sées
Chartres
Etampes
Troyes
St Brieuc
Les Clairets
Quimper
Rennes
Sens
Clairvaux
Le Mans
Orléans
Fleury
Pontigny
Langres
Vilaine
Montereau
Vannes
Loire
Beaulieu
Flavigny
Angers
Tours
Amboise
Vézelay
Dijon
Nantes
Fontevrault
Cher
Citeaux
Chinon
Loches
Bourges
Nevers
Autun
Thouars
FRANCE
La Ferté
Poitiers
Cluny
Saône
St Maixent
Charroux
Charlieu
La Rochelle
Vienne
Limoges
Clermont-Ferrand
Saintes
Angoulême
Ventadour
MASSIF
Allier
Périgueux
Brive-la-Gaillarde
Aurillac
Le Puy
Bordeaux
Dordogne
CENTRAL
Castillon
Garonne
Lot
Mende
Villandraut
Cahors
Bazas
Rodez
Agen
Moissac
Tarn
Albi
Uzès
Adour
La Couvertoirade
Nîmes
Dax
Lodève
Bayonne
Auch
Toulouse
Montpellier
Lescar
Scale 1 : 4 000 000
0   100 km
0   80 miles
Lourdes
Montaner
Carcassonne
Aude
Narbonne
PYRENEES
St Betrand

Mediterranean Sea

B   C   D

Right *The small village of La Couvertoirade, in southern France, was on one of the routes pilgrims took on their journey to the shrine of St James the Great at Compostela in northern Spain. This village, built on a rock, was taken by the Templar Knights in 1182. The knights built a castle there in the early 13th century. The Order of Templars was set up to protect pilgrims to the Holy Lands and to shrines in other lands. When the order was dissolved in 1312, La Couvertoirade passed to another order of knights — the Hospitalers, who defended the sick. The wall and towers you can see today were built in 1439. It is a fine example of a heavily fortified village.*

Below *An illustration from a French book about hunting,* The Book of the Hunt, *written in the late 14th century by Gaston Fébus, Count of Foix. Here the hunters, in the middle of whom sits the Count himself, prepare for a boar hunt.*

MEDIEVAL PARIS

THE MODERN CAPITAL CITY OF PARIS, France, takes its name from the Parisi tribe who lived in the area before the Romans invaded Gaul. The earliest occupation was on the largest of the islands in the River Seine which now flows through the city.

THE MEDIEVAL CAPITAL

From the 6th century onwards, Paris was gradually developed beyond the Roman walls and suburbs. Swamps around the River Seine were drained, monasteries built and the town became wealthy. The King of the Franks, Clovis, made Paris his capital in 508, and it became the permanent capital of France by the year 1000. The Cathedral of Notre Dame (Our Lady) was completed in the 14th century.

Much of medieval Paris was destroyed during the reign of Louis XIV in the 17th century and later when Napoleon III (Napoleon Bonaparte) built 60 new streets through the old town. These new wide streets were called boulevards.

Right Medieval Paris. The twin towers of the Cathedral of Notre Dame dominate this view of the Île de la Cité, the island in the middle of the River Seine connected to the rest of the city by bridges. Barges brought goods to wharfs around the island, and houses and shops lined the wooden bridges.

Below Paris during the 14th century. Nobles are attended by their servants in an illustration from Jean Froissart's accounts of life and war at the time. The city, crowded with houses and churches, is well protected by its wall, gates, and towers.

ITALY

U NTIL THE MIDDLE OF THE 6TH CENTURY Italy was still considered part of the Roman Empire. Then it was invaded by the Lombards in 568. It was unique in medieval Europe because the king of the Lombards was always a foreigner and after 774 had no authority over the whole of what we know as Italy today. In the 10th century it was under the control of the German rulers. Some of the northern cities – such as Venice, Milan, and Florence – remained independent.

FIVE MAJOR POWERS

The powerful kings of Aragon, based in Catalonia in northeast Spain, gradually acquired more and more territory to include the Balearic Islands and then the islands further east. In the 15th century they also took over the Kingdom of Naples.

By the early 15th century there were five major powers in Italy. The north was divided between the Duchy of Milan and the Venetian Republic. To the south the Republic of Florence was the strongest state in Tuscany. In the center lay the Papal State (of Rome, ruled by the pope) and further south the Kingdom of Naples.

POWERFUL FAMILIES AND REPUBLICS

In many territories power was held by committees of people elected to office – republics. This gradually changed as one powerful man, or family, emerged. For example, the Visconti family held Milan; the Medici took over the Republic of Florence; and Venice was ruled by a head of state, a *doge*, who was elected for life.

CONDOTTIERI (MERCENARIES)

Towns, republics, duchies, and kingdoms were often at war. Local troops, called the militia, protected most towns until the 14th century. A change then took place as towns bought the service of mercenary soldiers, called *condottieri*. They were often difficult to get rid of after the war, and towns were forced to continue paying for them – a sort of blackmail. One such mercenary was Bartolomeo Colleoni, captain-general of the army of Venice. Colleoni died a very rich man in 1476.

Below *This map of Rome was made in 1323 by Paolo di Venezia. It shows some of the monuments that would interest travelers, such as the walls of the city.*

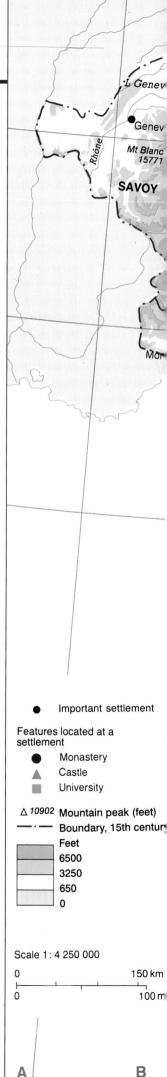

Important settlement

Features located at a settlement

- Monastery
- Castle
- University

△ 10902 Mountain peak (feet)

– ·– Boundary, 15th century

Feet
- 6500
- 3250
- 650
- 0

Scale 1 : 4 250 000

0 ——————— 150 km

0 ——————— 100 m

A   B

ITALY • SITES

SAN GIMIGNANO

TODAY SOME OF THE MOST IMPRESSIVE sights in Tuscany in northern Italy are the medieval fortified towns perched on hilltops. San Gimignano is one of these, with strongly built and easily defended towers. In 12th-century Italy there were many towns such as this that were independent and controlled the lands around. Each town needed strong defenses to fight off others that might claim its territory.

RULE BY THE PEOPLE

By the 13th century the "people" – the *popolo* – began to take over control of towns from the wealthy and powerful nobles who had run them before. The sort of people who now governed the towns were lawyers, merchants, and guilds of important industries, such as cloth manufacture. San Gimignano was like one great castle with a wall and towers protecting the limits of the town, and all the fields outside the walls. Also important in the town at this time was the *palazzo* – the residence of the town's government.

Above The Palazzo del Popolo was built in the 13th century as the headquarters of the town's chief magistrate.

Below San Gimignano once had 72 towers like these. The land around was known for its wine and grain production and was a center for the spice saffron.

FLORENCE

FLORENCE IS UNLIKE MANY OTHER TOWNS IN Tuscany because it is built on a flat plain. Its position is important, as it is built on both sides of the River Arno. The river was used for defense, trade, and communication.

FLORENCE IN THE 13TH CENTURY

Florence became very important in the 13th century because of the industries it developed. The town was famous for its cloth making, and the products were exported not only to other towns in Italy but also to France. By the late 13th century the town was governed by committees made up from members of its most powerful guilds, or associations, of professions and industries. The wealth created by these industries helped pay for the building of a wall to enclose the town, begun in about 1290.

GOVERNMENT BY THE FEW

The richer men who lent money to the city government in the 14th century eventually took

Below At the narrowest point of the River Arno is the Ponte Vecchio. A bridge has been here since the 10th century. This one, lined with shops, was rebuilt in 1345. It replaced one that was swept away in floods during 1333. Shops built along the side of the river emphasize the commercial importance of the river in Florence.

control of the city's affairs. Only in the 15th century did one family, the Medici, become the ruling family. Florence, already wealthy, began to conquer other major towns around, such as Arezzo in 1385 and Pisa in 1406.

THE BUILDINGS OF FLORENCE

Florence was just as famous for its art and architecture as it was for its trade and industries. The wealth created from its industries paid for many of the fine buildings, such as the Palazzo Vecchio, which we can still see today.

It was not only architects who found employment in Florence. The town had many other artists, sculptors, masons, glaziers, painters, and goldsmiths. They helped decorate the many churches and public buildings of the city.

SCHOOLS AND A UNIVERSITY

The towns of Tuscany, Florence in particular, were well known for their schools. Standards of literacy were high, and the great Italian poet Dante (1265–1321), who wrote the *Divine Comedy*, was a Florentine. But for training in law and in medicine it was necessary to go to the greater universities, such as Bologna. In Florence, from the late 14th and 15th centuries, some of the leading citizens encouraged the rediscovery of Greek classics and their study.

Below Towering above the medieval buildings of Florence is its duomo — cathedral — *which was begun in 1296 but not consecrated as a cathedral until 1436. It is called Santa Maria del Fiore (Saint Mary of the Flower). Two parts of the cathedral stand out above the main body of the church. The great cupola or dome was begun in 1420, and the campanile (bell-tower) covered in marble was finished in 1387.*

GENOA

THE TRADING TOWN OF GENOA HAD ONE very important advantage over some of its rivals — a good natural harbor. It had new markets opened to it with the success of the First Crusade in the 11th century. The wealth from its trade allowed the town to grow and develop both its harbor and its defenses.

INTERNATIONAL TRADE

Genoa's position on the northwest coast of Italy meant that trade links were developed especially

Below The Porta Soprana, with its two towers, is part of   the city wall built around Genoa in 1155.

with western Europe and Africa. Cloth was the most important import from other towns in Italy and from Germany and Spain. In return, Genoa traded dyes from the East, spices, perfumes, and precious stones. Genoa established trading posts in Africa as bases for its merchants.

TRADING RIVALRIES

Genoa's nearest rival was Pisa. In 1284 Genoa defeated Pisa in battle and gained control of the town's trade links. Its other rival, Venice — on the east coast of Italy — was more difficult to beat. Venice had set up its trade links in the East very early on and had a monopoly in Constantinople. Genoa founded posts in Asia Minor (now Turkey) to import alum, which was needed to fix dyes in cloth.

TRADE

F EW COMMUNITIES CAN EXIST SIMPLY ON what they can produce themselves. People usually have to import goods — extra food, clothes, and equipment, for example — from elsewhere. Goods might have to be brought from the next village or a nearby town. But some items have to be carried vast distances. In medieval times, areas and towns came to specialize in particular goods, such as the woolen industry in Flanders. Most important towns grew as trading centers rather than as places where goods were made — towns such as Venice, London, Bruges, and Genoa.

PROTECTING THE TRADE ROUTES

Those who traded — the merchants — had to arrange for their own goods to be fetched and protected. There were many dangers. For example, piracy was a real problem in northern Europe in the 13th century. There was no overall law to protect all Europe as there had been in the Roman period.

The great center of trade in the medieval period was the Mediterranean. The Crusades made it possible for pilgrims and merchants to travel to the East and so helped trade develop.

Below European trade in the 14th century. Most trade was carried out by sea. Not all overland routes are shown, but notice how many make use of rivers — to Paris and Toledo (in Spain) for example. Some areas developed their natural resources for trade (such as wine or metals), while others became centers for particular trades (cloth making, for example).

Textile making areas
- Cloth
- Linen
- Fustian (rough cotton)
- Silk

— Trade route

▼ Metalworking center
▲ Important fair
● Other settlement

Location of commodity
- ● Cotton
- ● Fruit
- ● Gold
- ● Grain
- ◆ Leather
- ◆ Spices
- ◆ Sugar
- ■ Timber
- ■ Wine
- ■ Wool

Scale 1 : 20 000 000

0   600 km

0   400 miles

LAND ROUTES AND SEA ROUTES

Great fairs were held all over Europe to exchange goods. At first most trade was carried out by merchants using pack animals. This meant slow journeys with the threat of attacks by robbers. It also meant that only small quantities of goods could be carried. By the 14th century ships were increasingly used for trade. Large quantities of goods, such as grain for bread, could be shipped from, say, Sicily to feed the townspeople of Bruges or Antwerp.

TRADING NATIONS

Important items of trade included cloth, timber, and some foodstuffs such as grain and wine. Two Italian towns in particular established themselves as great centers of trade. Genoa was well placed to trade both inland to northern Europe and by sea in the western and eastern Mediterranean. And the government in Venice was able to use its harbors to establish many trade routes.

Throughout the eastern Mediterranean you can still see Venetian forts that helped protect their trade routes. There are many on mainland Greece and its islands, in particular on Crete.

Left Guilds (or associations) of trades and crafts were common from the 13th century. Members of the guild of cloth merchants in Bologna, Italy, are shown here filling a street with their stalls and booths.

Below Genoa, Italy, was one of the earliest cities known for its money changers or bankers from the 12th century. Here the bankers are counting coins to give to the town's widows and orphans.

THE BRITISH ISLES

Many of the fields and roads that can be seen in Britain today were well established long before the Romans conquered the country in 43 CE. Since then many different peoples have made changes to the map of Britain. The names of places, for example, can often be traced to the later invasions of Anglo-Saxon, Viking, or Norman settlers.

ENGLISH BOUNDARIES ESTABLISHED

By the 13th century England was a kingdom and could properly be called one country. It was no longer as closely linked to France as it had been before. The king had established a parliament to advise him. The king sent for powerful people to represent different parts of the country. They came from the shires (for example, Oxfordshire or Yorkshire) and from important towns (such as Rochester). Smaller units in the country, the ecclesiastical parishes, had been established before the Norman invasion and continued to run local affairs.

ROYAL AND CHURCH LANDS AND PORTS

Even at this time some lands remained totally in the hands of either the king or the church, as the map shows. Five south-coast ports, called the Cinque Ports (*cinq* is French for "five"), had special privileges and duties. They provided ships for the navy in return for tax allowances.

WALES AND THE KING

The situation in Wales was different. No one prince was strong enough to dominate the whole country. When the princes of Gwynedd in the north tried to do this they were stopped by an alliance between King Edward I of England and some of the other Welsh princes. After 1284 King Edward took over the government of Gwynedd himself and built a number of castles there.

IRELAND

Although King Henry II claimed the lordship of Ireland and many Norman lords were established there, the English never gained control of the whole of the island. Very few English kings ever went there. By 1485 the English really controlled only an area known as the Pale around Dublin. The boundaries of medieval Ireland underwent significant changes in more recent times.

Left One of the best places to see what an English medieval town was like is York in the north of the country. This is the area known as the Shambles where wooden buildings overhang the street to gain as much floor space as possible. Most of the buildings have now been restored.

Below Ireland has been a Christian country since the 5th century. Christian crosses, like this one at Castledermot, were built in many places. This is one of 50 that still survive from before the 9th century. It is highly carved and shows the suffering of Christ.

Left The Angel Choir inside the cathedral at Lincoln, a town of about 4,000 people in the Norman period. The cathedral was begun in the late 11th century. The Normans built four cathedrals, which were served by canons (see pages 42–43). There were already nine in Britain during the Saxon period. Lincoln Cathedral was gradually enlarged and completed in the late 14th century.

Settlements
◆ Cinque port
● Important town

Features located at a settlement
● Monastery
▲ Castle
■ University

–·–·– Boundary, 13th century
——— Pale boundary

Feet
1625
650
0

Scale 1 : 4 000 000
0   100 km
0   80 miles

Outer Hebrides
The Minch
Dunskeath
Dunvegan
Skye
Inverness   Nairn
Eileen Donan   *Spey*
Banff
Inner Hebrides
GRAMPIAN MTS
Dee
Aberdeen
Inverey
Mull
SCOTLAND
Iona
Tay
Forfar
North Sea
Perth
Abernethy
Stirling
Islay
North Berwick
Tarbert
Paisley   Edinburgh
Rutherglen   Berwick
Tweed
Ayr   Roxburgh
Clyde   Alnwick
Dunaverty
Holywood   Hermitage
Tyne
Wigtown   Newcastle
Carlisle   Durham
Londonderry
Carrickfergus
Mourne   Appleby
Lough Neagh   Richmond   Scarborough
Assaroe   Inch   PENNINES
Armagh   *Ouse*
Killala   *Isle of Man*   Lancaster
Boyle   IRELAND   Dundalk   York
Roscommon   Clitheroe
L Corrib   PALE   *Irish Sea*
Athlone   Trim   ENGLAND
Galway   *Shannon*   Dublin
Barrow   Lincoln
Suir   Castledermot   Beaumaris   Conway   Chester   Tattershall
Limerick   Kilkenny   Caernarvon   Newcastle-under-Lyme
Ardfert   Clonmel   *Trent*   Nottingham
Blackwater   Harlech   CAMBRIAN MTS   Shrewsbury   Peterborough   Norwich
Waterford   Bere   Bridgnorth   *Nene*
Cork   WALES   Warwick   Cambridge   Bury St Edmunds
St George's Channel   Hereford   Bedford
St David's   Dynevor   *Severn*   Gloucester   Colchester
Pembroke   Oxford   St Albans
Llandaff   Windsor   *Thames*   London
Devizes   Rochester   Sandwich
Canterbury   Dover
Glastonbury   Salisbury   Winchester   Hythe
Exe   Arundel   Romney
Porchester   Hastings
Exeter   Corfe
Truro   *English Channel*

North Channel

A   B   C   D   1   2   3   4   5

CASTLES

THE WORD FOR A CASTLE IN MEDIEVAL
Latin was *castrum* or *castellum*. "Castle" is
often used for any fortified place; the Latin
word was used by the Romans for a military fort.
Other, later peoples made fortifications, of course.
The Saxons, for example, fortified their towns
against the Danes and called them *burhs*. There is a
burh at Dover, on the southern coast of Britain, but
castles of later periods have been built on top of it.

BUILT BY THE POWERFUL

A castle was a safe place. It had to be secure against
attack and a last resort for the regular inhabitants
and often the people who lived around it. The site
of a castle had to be carefully chosen. The best
places were often already defended simply by the
landscape – on a high ridge or with sheer cliffs on
one side, for example. To build a castle you had to
be powerful and you had to be rich.

The king often built a number of castles to hold
power over the land. King Edward I of England,
for example, built eight new castles in Wales from
1277 to 1304 in an attempt to control the whole
of this country. However, the king could not
control all his territory alone. He gave some land
away to those he could trust. In France the king
granted lands and the right to control them. These
were called fiefs. In return the barons or the knights
gave the king their loyalty and supplied him with
fighting men.

CASTLES OF TIMBER AND EARTH

In some parts of Europe the first castles built in
the 10th century were made of timber (for walls,
gates, and buildings inside) and earth (for the outer
defenses, for example). In 11th-century England
they were called motte-and-bailey castles.

A great mound (motte) of earth was constructed
and a wooden building put on top. This was the
keep or strongest point in the castle. Around it was
the bailey – an area surrounded by walls of earth
and timber – where the people lived. Some castles
had an inner bailey (around the keep) and an outer
bailey, also protected by a wall and guard towers.

BUILDING IN STONE

In England after 1150 very few timber-and-earth
castles were built. Stone could provide a much
stronger and more permanent building. This type
of building was very expensive though. The stone
castle at Dover built in the late 12th century cost

about £7,000. This was a huge sum of money in
those times. Building in stone allowed the architects
to develop better ideas for making the castle a safe
place to live in. At Dover the 82ft-high stone keep
was surrounded by a courtyard which was protected
by a high wall with guard towers.

Castles were built to protect the interests of a
particular lord or king or to provide a garrison for
soldiers. But they were also for living in. The castle
was the fortified home not only for the knight but
also for his family, his servants, his craftspeople,
and his fighting men. In times of trouble the bailey
courtyard, already full of buildings and animals,
became the temporary home of villagers around.

Left Curemonte Castle in
Brive la Gaillarde in France is
actually two castles joined by a
surrounding wall with round
towers built in the 14th century.

Below Reconstruction drawing
of the motte at Abinger, Surrey,
in England. The mound, built
by the Normans in the 11th
century, had a timber
watchtower on top.

Below The castle at
Frangocastello, Crete, built by
the Venetians to protect their
trade routes in 1371.

Above The Normans first built a castle at Rochester in Kent soon after the Battle of Hastings in 1066. A motte-and-bailey castle defended the crossing of the River Medway. The later stone castle on the same site, and the great cathedral, as above, were begun by Bishop Gundulf in about 1087.

Right The keep of Rochester Castle is one of the largest in England. This huge building, with its three floors and roof battlements, was begun in 1127. There are no doors at ground level — attackers had to get past the guard tower and portcullis. On various floors there are bedrooms, halls for eating in, lavatories, and a chapel. A well inside the keep provided fresh water.

THE COUNTRYSIDE

ODAY IN EUROPE MOST PEOPLE GO TO THE supermarket for their daily food. Some of that food may come from the land around the town or village, but most will come from further away, from foreign countries. Medieval people living in the countryside ate only what they produced on their own land.

In most European countries medieval kings claimed control over the land but allowed trusted lords the rights to much of it. The lords of estates relied on tenants to work the land and collected either rents or produce each year.

USING ALL THE LAND'S RESOURCES

The amount of land an ordinary family was able to work varied from country to country and from place to place. In England a family with about 12 hectares (30 acres) to plow could probably live quite well from what food they could produce. Other families had to make do with half of that.

Besides growing their crops, people had the right to graze their animals on meadows and rough land. Most people had a few animals such as sheep, pigs, and chickens and an ox or a horse for plowing. People also had the right to collect other things from the land – turf for roofing and to burn, wood, nuts and berries, and bracken for beds and for animal food.

HUNTING AND FISHING

For country people trying to live off the land, the right to fish, catch eels and frogs or net birds was

essential. In some parts of Europe hunting animals in forests provided a ready source of food. Fish was an important part of the medieval diet. Monasteries, castles, and manor houses usually had their own ponds to ensure a regular supply of fresh fish.

For the wealthy, hunting was a sport to enjoy and an important way to keep healthy and in good shape for warfare. Hunting areas were protected and guarded, both from scavenging animals and from those without the right to hunt. There were inhumane penalties for any people who were caught poaching.

Left Hunting with falcons was a popular sport for the well-born. Notice that the handlers are wearing strong leather gauntlets. The illustration comes from a book on the subject of falconry made in the mid-13th century for Manfred, King of Sicily.

Right This illustration from a French book was made in about 1411 to illustrate the month of March. Pictures like this add to our evidence about life in the countryside gathered from archeological work and from documents. The fields are small, and the man in the foreground is plowing with two oxen. Fields were often divided into strips and the strips allotted to the villagers so that each family had some good and some poor land to work. In the field further back, workers are pruning vines for the wine harvest.

Left Refreshment was not forgotten after a day's hunting – notice the dogs, horses, and hunting horns. This illustration and the one on the right are from The Book of the Hunt by Gaston Fébus written in 1387 in France.

Right Gaston Fébus was an expert on hunting stag and boar using dogs. He also used nets, for trapping hares and foxes. Nets of rope are being made here. Much finer nets were used for catching all types of birds – from songbirds to pigeons.

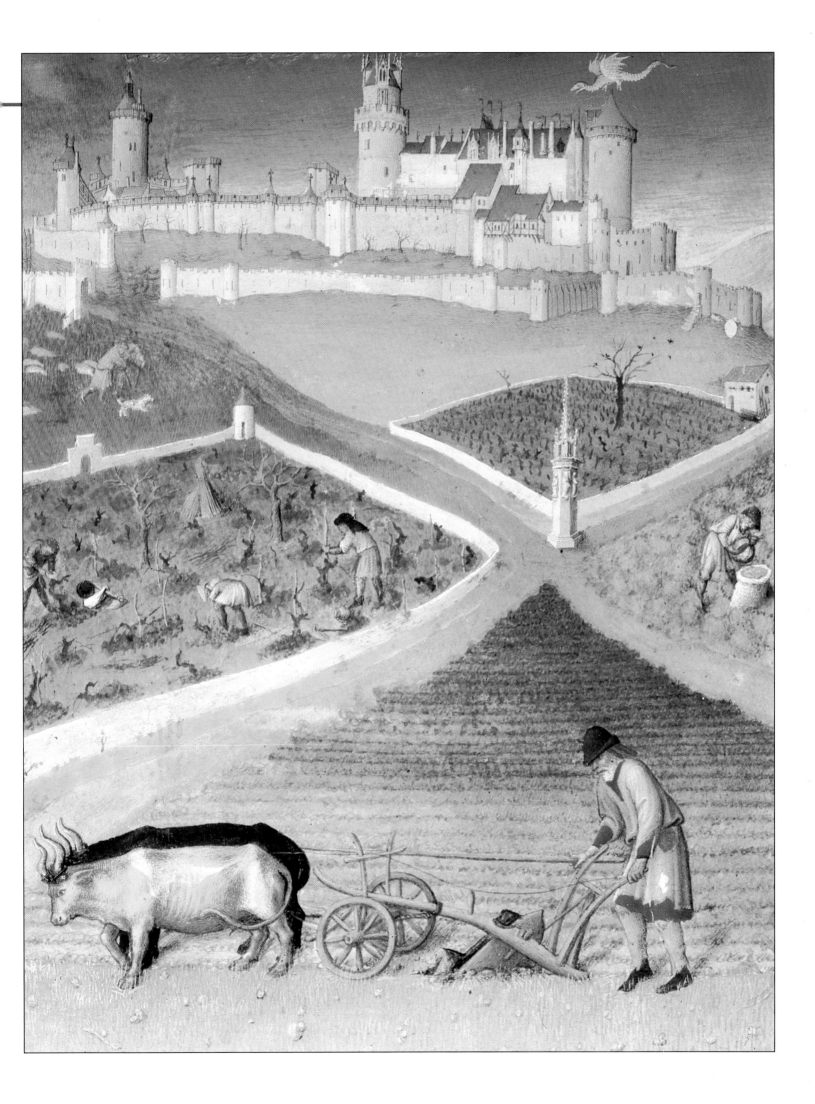

SPAIN AND PORTUGAL

Part of the story of medieval Europe is the struggle between two great religious faiths – Christianity and Islam. Much of this struggle took place in the area later known as Spain and Portugal.

AN ISLAMIC MEDITERRANEAN

At the time of the death of the Islamic prophet Muhammad in 632, the Muslims controlled the area of Arabia on the eastern side of the Red Sea. Throughout the 7th century they moved north into the Holy Land and east along the Persian Gulf and Arabian Sea. They also conquered North Africa, reaching Ceuta (near Gibraltar) in 709. From here they struck out into Europe. By 750 the Muslims occupied Portugal, most of Spain and part of southern France.

THE CHRISTIANS GAIN CONTROL

Although the Christians held a small amount of territory in the north of Spain, it was not until the middle of the 11th century that they had much success against Muslim occupation. They called this fight the *Reconquista*, or reconquest. Most reconquest took place either in the late 11th century or in the early part of the 13th century. Land was taken away from the Muslims and given to the new conquerors, but Muslims were allowed to live in the new kingdoms, at least until the 16th century.

Below The town of Avila in the kingdom of Castile, now Spain. Its impressive town walls were put up after the town had been reconquered from the Muslims in the late 11th century. The walls are 40ft high, defended by huge round towers and eight gates. The town had originally been founded by the Romans, and a lot of Roman buildings were reused to make the fortifications.

Settlements
◆ Christian center
● Important town

Features located at a settlement
● Monastery
▲ Castle
■ University

—·— Boundary, 14th century

Bay of Biscay

CANTABRIAN MOUNTAINS

PYRENEES

Ebro

León

Santander

Covadonga

San Sebastian

Pamplona

NAVARRE

Leyre

San Juan de la Peña

Sahagún

Huelgas

Burgos

Calahorra

Huesca

Alquézar

Ripoll

Besalú

Gerona

Palencia

Arlaniza

Fitero

Ebro

Cinca

Lérida

Montserrat

Valderaduey

Soria

Tarazona

Saragossa

Poblet

Santa Creus

Barcelona

Zamora

Duero

Valladolid

Peñafiel

Osma

Jalón

Piedra

Cáspe

Tarragona

a del Campo

Coca

Segovia

SIERRA DE GUADARRAMA

SERRANIA

DE CUENCA

Albarracín

ARAGON

Tortosa

Salamanca

Avila

S Geronimo de Yuste

Madrid

Alcalá

CASTILE

Tagus

Cuenca

Segorbe

Agal

Toledo

Turia

Guadalupe

Alcázar de San Juan

Valencia

Guadiana

Júcar

Ciudad Real

Chinchilla

San Martin

Alicante

Baños de la Encina

Segura

Baeza

Murcia

Córdoba

Guadalquivir

Jaén

Cartagena

lá de Guadaira

Genil

Santafé

Granada

GRANADA

SIERRA NEVADA

Almería

Málaga

Gibraltar

Above *The northern town of Alquézar was founded by the Muslims but captured by the Spanish in 1087.*

Ciudadela

Minorca

Palma

Balearic Islands

Majorca

Feet

6500

3250

650

0

Scale 1 : 3 400 000

0   150 km

0   100 miles

C   D   E

Mapmaking

THE EARLIEST MAPS WE KNOW OF IN THE world were made by the Babylonians in the Near East in about 2300 BCE. The Greeks also made maps, and it was to these that the first medieval mapmakers referred.

Ptolemy – Greek mapmaker

Ptolemy, who was from the Greek city of Alexandria in Egypt, wrote his work *Geography* in the 2nd century. Copies were made in the 13th century, and the book was translated into Latin in 1406.

Below "EVROPA MVNDI PARS QVARTA" – *"Europe a quarter of the world." Part of a book written in Latin in about 1120, called* Liber Floridus. *The author thought that the world was divided into four quarters of a circle.*

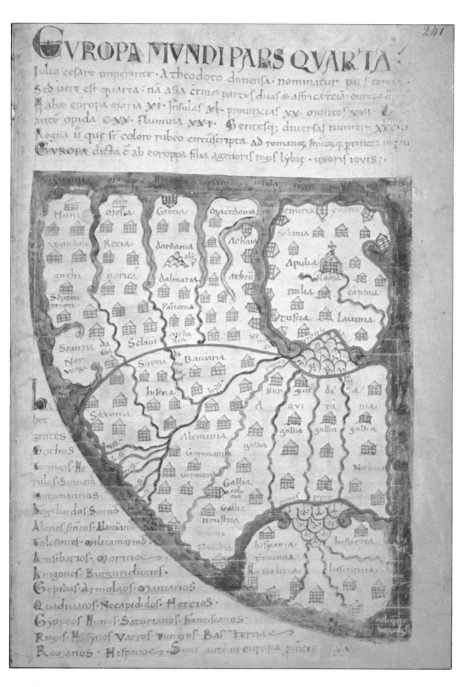

Sea charts and atlases

Ptolemy's work, together with specially drawn maps, was printed in Italy in 1477. But there had been new detailed maps in Europe before that, in the 13th century, used mainly as a help for navigation at sea. The magnetic compass had been known as an aid since the late 12th century. These sea charts, the compass, and the astrolabe (see page 48) required a knowledge of mathematics to work out the right course. The earliest atlas that survives today was made for King Charles V of France in 1375.

Above A picture map of Inglemoor, England, made in 1405. It shows points of the compass, rivers, bridges, villages, fields, and the moor itself in the center. It was drawn for a court hearing when ownership of the land was disputed.

Specialized maps

Specialized maps and charts were produced in the 14th century for traders from centers such as Venice and Genoa. The Mediterranean world was very well mapped. For example, in 1320 Marino Sanudo, from Venice, wrote about the problem of conquering the Holy Land from the Muslims and sent his book to the Pope with a set of maps made by Pietro Visconte.

Maps of the world

In the 15th century the invention of printing meant that maps could easily be produced from woodcuts or from copper plates. It was in this century that voyages of discovery were made and new maps of the wider world had to be produced. The Portuguese were the first people in Europe to set sail for new lands across seas that had never been charted before.

Below This sea chart of part of western Europe was made in 1497 by Freducci d'Ancona. Each country is easily recognizable today, and the coastlines have been accurately plotted. Compare this map with the modern one of Europe on pages 8–9. Here the interior of the countries is not plotted in detail – for example, Paris and London are not shown.

Left Cartographers (map- and chart-makers) at work on a coastline from their ship. The west coast of Africa was plotted by a cartographer from Venice in 1448, but the Portuguese captains sent out by Prince Henry the Navigator had reached this coast 17 years before.

JOURNEY TO COMPOSTELA

PILGRIMAGES WERE VERY POPULAR IN medieval Europe. People so treasured the remains and possessions of the many saints that they believed they could be healed by them. Pilgrims also made their long journeys in the hope that their sins would be forgiven.

DANGEROUS JOURNEYS

Many pilgrims probably thought that the danger of long-distance travel was punishment enough for their sins. Jerusalem was one place that was much visited, but when the Muslims conquered the city in 638 other shrines became popular. From the 11th century parties of pilgrims were organized, such as the one described in Chaucer's *Canterbury Tales*.

THE SHRINE OF ST JAMES

The more important shrines were those of the Apostles of Christ. People believed the tomb discovered in about 830 at Compostela in northern Spain was that of St James the Apostle. A church was built there, and pilgrims from Spain began making the journey. The news of the shrine soon spread. At the end of the 11th century the Pope ordered the bishop of the region Iria to move his headquarters there.

There were four main pilgrim routes from France to Compostela, though people also came there from further away. Along the routes monasteries were built, and villages and towns became wealthy from the pilgrim trade.

Right Three of the main pilgrim routes across France came together at Ostabat. In medieval times it was prosperous and catered for large numbers of travelers. Now Ostabat is a quiet village.

Right This church at Conques, France, was built in the mid-11th century on the route from Le Puy to Ostabat. At Conques a local child saint was revered — St Foy.

Below At Santillana, on the northern coast of Spain, this church was built in the Romanesque style. This style of architecture was popular in the late 11th and 12th centuries and copied ideas from Rome.

Above Legends about St James arose late in the medieval period. They were probably based less on fact than on people's need to believe in miracles and wonders.

Marne

Paris

Chartres

Seine

Yonne

Orléans

Auxerre

Vézelay

Loire

Tours

Bourges

Nevers

Allier

Loire

Poitiers

Le Puy

Rhône

Aulnay

St Jean-d'Angély

Limoges

St Léonard-de-Noblat

Clermont-Ferrand

Saintes

FRANCE

Blaye

Périgueux

Bergerac

Dordogne

Aurillac

Rocamadour

Bordeaux

Garonne

Conques

Belin

Lot

Cahors

Agen

Moissac

Nîmes

Arles

Aix

Montpellier

St Gilles

Bay of Biscay

St Sever

Adour

Aire

Auch

Toulouse

Sorde

Santillana

Santander

San Sebastian

Ostabat

SPAIN

Guernica

Valcarlos

St Jean-Pied-de-Port

Cize Pass

Roncesvalles

Somport Pass

PYRENEES

Pamplona

Monreal

Canfranc

Mediterranean Sea

Santo Domingo de la Calzada

Puente de la Reina

Aragon

Jaca

Sahagun

Los Arcos

Sanguesa

rrion

Tardajos

Burgos

Logroño

Najera

Castrogeriz

Villafranca

mista

Palencia

Huesca

Ebro

Legend:
- ● Monastery
- ● Town or village visited by pilgrims
- ✕ Mountain pass
- ▨ Land over 3250 feet
- — Approximate route taken by pilgrims

Scale 1 : 3 500 000

0 _____ 100km

0 _____ 75 miles

CENTRAL EUROPE

SOME PARTS OF MEDIEVAL EUROPE DEVELOPED quite separate histories, which were not connected with the establishment of the large Roman Empire. However, the German Empire or Holy Roman Empire looked back to Rome and tried to reestablish some of its traditions.

DEVELOPMENT OF AN EMPIRE

"The Empire," as it was known, was not completely controlled by one emperor. The 14th century was a period of great change in medieval Europe and in the German Empire a number of families held power. Two families in particular ruled this Empire: the Luxembourg family from 1346 to 1437 and then the Hapsburgs from 1438 onwards. However, a number of separate states and cities that declared themselves "free" also made up the Empire.

GOVERNING A LARGE TERRITORY

Some noble families claimed the throne of the Empire, and wars frequently went on between powerful groups. However, the emperor had to be elected by princes and had to influence them and the independent cities and states in order to remain in overall control.

SWITZERLAND

This area in particular shows the complicated way in which the Empire was formed and governed. Switzerland had been part of the territory of the German Empire since the 11th century and was ruled by a number of noble families. During the 13th century the number of Swiss towns rose from 16 to 80. In 1291 a confederation of independent districts and prosperous towns joined together. Their independence showed that Switzerland was powerful and not afraid to use its army to resist the German princes. Switzerland was nevertheless part of the German Empire.

THE LOW COUNTRIES

Another example of the complicated nature of the Empire can be seen in the countries which bordered the North Sea. Flanders had been part of the French kingdom but passed into the territory of the dukes of Burgundy, who also took over Brabant in 1404. In fact by the middle part of the 15th century the dukes of Burgundy had become very rich and powerful. They held land from the Swiss border north to Holland and built up Antwerp as a trading port.

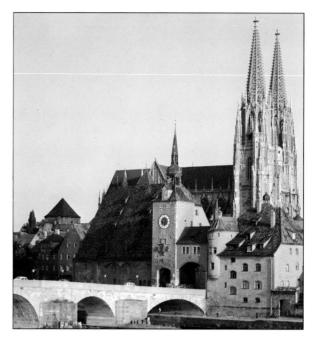

Above The 12th-century stone bridge across the Danube at the cathedral city of Regensburg, Germany.

Right Toplerschlösschen im Rosenthal. This fortified German tower guards the town's mills.

Below Rothenburg and its town walls were rebuilt in the 14th century.

North Sea

● Boulog

● Am

Au

Nevers

Settlements

■ Hanse town (see also pages 88–89)

○ Independent city

● Important town

Features located at a settlement

● Monastery

▲ Castle

■ University

△ 15781 Mountain peak (feet)

—·— Boundary, 14–15th centuries

Feet
6500
3250
650
0
Below sea level

Scale 1 : 5 500 000

0   150 km

0   100 miles

A

EVERYDAY LIFE

For very many people in medieval Europe life was hard – perhaps harder for those living in towns than for those in the countryside. Despite much poverty and disease, the population rose quickly. We think that there were about 22½ million inhabitants of western Europe in 950. By the middle of the 14th century this number had doubled.

TOWNS

Although most people lived in the country, more towns grew up in the medieval period. By our standards now they were not very big. The larger towns, such as Hamburg and London, each had between some 20,000 and 40,000 inhabitants by the 14th century. There were more than 100,000 people in only a very few cities, such as Paris, Milan, and Venice. Town and countryside were not separated in quite the way they are today. Many townspeople cultivated gardens and fields and kept animals inside the town's walls.

EVIDENCE ABOUT EVERYDAY LIFE

While we have some evidence about the lives of ordinary people from documents and pictures, we can also find out a great deal from the results of archeological work. For example, we can look at leather shoes preserved by being thrown into a well when they were worn out. Everyone in the medieval world used pottery to store things in, to cook with and to eat from. Pottery fragments survive very well. Some of the most interesting evidence comes from wooden carvings, often found on church seats, which were being made as early as the 13th century.

INDUSTRY

Industry was usually carried out in towns. Specialized workshops (not factories) were established, often in the place where the raw material was to be found. For example, we know that there was pottery production in Cologne in Germany by at least the 8th century. Much of the work was done by hand. Craftsmen carved animal bone and horn into everyday objects such as counters for games, combs, buttons, and even ice skates. But machines were introduced where possible, to help with production. Spinning wheels and clocks were both medieval inventions. In the countryside wind- and watermills provided power. Watermills were used for sawing wood, making cloth, and making paper, for example.

Above Humorous wooden carving from the church at Fairford, England, showing a husband being battered by his wife. It is on a misericord, or "mercy seat" – a ledge cut under a tip-up seat to allow the clergy to take the weight off their feet during long church services.

Left Inside a German kitchen the housewife or housekeeper (notice the bunch of keys) cooks over a wood fire. In the iron cauldron is the daily pottage, or soup-stew, made from vegetables and meat.

Below and right Guilds often paid for stained-glass windows in churches (right). A drapers' (cloth makers') guild had these made showing carding (combing) the cloth and cutting the nap (the rough surface).

There were many small industries in towns, places for shops and where goods could be traded (below). This scene is of a German town in the early 16th century.

GUILDS

Often, groups of specialized workers formed themselves into guilds — made up from masters who ran the shops of workmen. Each laid down rules for the way they worked, traded, and trained new workers (the apprentices). Guild rules always stressed the importance of the members' religious duties. Like similar associations today, they also looked after their members and their members' families in times of trouble or hardship. Guilds played an important part in the running and government of some towns and could be very powerful.

SOUTHEASTERN EUROPE

THE AREA COVERED IN THE MAP ON THE right is vast – roughly 11 times the size of England. The history of this area in the medieval period is the most complicated in Europe. There were two main aspects to this history. One was the continuing involvement in this area of western European kings, states, and cities. The other was the gradual increase in the size of the Muslim Empire under the Ottoman Turks.

THE OTTOMAN THREAT

The Ottoman Turks, at the beginning of the 14th century, held only a small amount of land on the southern edge of the Black Sea. Through the 14th and 15th centuries they were able to gain control of Asia Minor, Greece, and part of the Balkans. They took Constantinople, the capital of the Eastern Empire, in 1453. These Muslim Turks were dedicated soldiers. Their huge and effective armies had little difficulty in overcoming the divided forces of the western European princes who opposed them.

GREECE AND THE BALKANS

There were many groups in this area to fight the Muslim advance, but often they fought each other as well. The Order of the Knights of St John defended the island of Rhodes against the Muslims. The Venetians and the Genoese held territory in Greece and Asia Minor. Their occupation held back the Muslims, but these two cities were more interested in trade than in establishing a new Christian empire in the East. For much of the 14th century, in fact, they fought each other.

Other western groups were interested in this part of the world, but their military power was limited. The King of Aragon acquired Sicily in 1282, and then in the 14th century Catalans took Athens and a large area around it. For a time the French controlled some lands in Greece and northwards as far as Hungary. The situation changed often.

BOHEMIA

To the north of the area fought over by Muslims and Christians was the powerful kingdom of Bohemia. The mountains of Bohemia provided Europe with much of its basic supplies of gold and silver. The Czechs, Bohemia's most influential people, were ruled by their own kings until the 14th century. By then the king of Bohemia held the most important position in central Europe. Bohemia took over a number of neighboring states, including Hungary and Lausitz. The ruler of the German Empire was elected by the king of Bohemia and six German princes. The first university of the German Empire was founded in Prague in 1348. At one time in the early 14th century the kings of Bohemia even ruled Poland.

Left The finely decorated west front of the abbey at Ják in western Hungary. This is 13th-century architecture, dating from the rebuilding of the abbey after the invasion of the Mongol hordes in 1241.

Below The castle and defensive walls of the Knights of St John on the island of Rhodes. The knights, driven out from Acre in the Holy Land, crusaded against the Muslims from Rhodes from 1310 to 1522.

NORTHEASTERN EUROPE

THE TWO MOST IMPORTANT STATES IN THE far eastern part of medieval Europe were Poland and Russia. In between these two great states stood Lithuania, which emerged as a separate state in the 13th century and by the end of the 14th century was combined with Poland under a Lithuanian king.

POLAND

The name Poland comes from a Slavonic word, *pole*, meaning a field or plain. Its people were *poleni* – the inhabitants of the fields. Unlike in other areas of medieval Europe, here the territories controlled by tribes were joined together as a state quite early on in history. The first ruler was Mieszko I, who governed from 963 to 992. Soon after he took over he was converted to Christianity, and Poland became a Catholic state accepting the authority of the pope in Rome.

Mieszko established the Piast dynasty (ruling family) although he had to pay homage to the powerful German emperor. Poland did not survive long as one unified state. In the 12th century the land was ruled by a number of dukes but was reunited in the 14th century.

RUSSIA

The land we know today as Russia developed in quite a different way. In the 10th century the cities around Kiev were linked together under the rule of descendants of merchant-soldiers who had come from Scandinavia. For a long time communities, whose wealth came from agriculture not trade, ruled themselves but they were overrun by the Mongol hordes from the Far East in the early 13th century.

After this the Russians were divided into two main groups – the Great Russians and the White Russians. The Great Russians, whose power-base was the growing city of Moscow, emerged as the stronger group in the 13th and 14th centuries.

Below Krakow in Poland was an important city in the development of the country. It became the headquarters (called the "seat") of the bishop in about 1000. The cathedral shown here was built in about 1018 but rebuilt in the 14th century. Krakow university was established in 1364.

Above Icons – images of God, Christ, and the saints – were an important part of Russian Orthodox Christianity. This icon was made in the 14th century in Novgorod, in western Russia, and shows the Trinity with God as the father and the child Christ.

- ● Important settlement

Features located at a settlement
- ● Monastery
- ■ University

- –·–·– Boundary, 14th century

Feet
3250
650
0

Scale 1 : 9 000 000

0 ___ 200km

0 ___ 150 miles

Baltic Sea

Marienwalde
Poznan
Warthe
Ploc
Wschowa
Lodz
POLAND
Radomsko
Krakow
Stary S.

A

Lake Onega

Kargopol

Velikii Ustyug

Lake Ladoga

Sukhona

Staroladozhskii

Ferapontov

Gulf of Finland

Neva

Oreshek

Blagoveschenskii

Kirov

Volkhov

Vologda

RUSSIA

Galich

Shcheremenskii

Novgorod

Borovich

Krasnokholmskii

Unzha

Lovat

Yaroslavl

Volga

Nikolaevskii Tikhonov

Kholm

Torzhok

Rostov

Gorodets

Volga

Tver

Suzdal

Nizhnii Novgorod
Volga

Braslav

Moscow

Murom

Polotsk

Dvina

Vilna

Gzhatsk

Oka

Neman

Dnieper

Smolensk

CENTRAL

Ryazan

Grodno

RUSSIAN

Kaluga

Don

Minsk

Kirov

Novogrudok

Mogilev

UPLANDS

Odoyev

Wizha

Dankov

LITHUANIA

Yelets

saw

Brest

ka

Pripet

Turov

Lublin

Wlodximierz

Desna

Lutsk

Chernigov

Kiev

Bjelgorod

Lvov

Poltava

Halicz

Dnieper

Dniester

Bug

B

C

D

4

3

2

1

A RUSSIAN VILLAGE

THE SCENE BELOW OF A MEDIEVAL VILLAGE in Russia has been reconstructed from a number of different sources. Some buildings do survive, and there are drawings in manuscripts that also have written descriptions of village life.

SETTING THE SCENE

It was not until very recently that people living in towns and country villages could avoid the mud and slush caused by unpaved roads. In winter the stoves in the houses provided the only warmth.

BUILDINGS OF WOOD

Medieval houses, all across Europe, were built using wood. But Russian villages and towns were built almost completely of wood – even Moscow, which became known as the Wooden City. Split tree trunks were laid to make the tracks usable. The houses were made of logs, and fire was the greatest hazard. Here, the chapel is also constructed from wood, even the roof. There was a great deal of very elaborate wood carving on some buildings, as on the little dome in our illustration. The cross standing on its own is also made of wood.

Below In this scene, the
boyar's weapons and the means
of transport were inherited from
the Mongols. The Mongols, as
skilled warrior horsemen,
overran northern China, north
India and Russia as far west as
the Black Sea. Their influence in
Russia lasted until the end of the
medieval period.

PEOPLE AND TRAVEL

It was obviously difficult to travel in such
conditions. In Russia the sledge was very useful,
especially over frozen ground and iced-over rivers.
In the illustration, the central figure on horseback is
a *boyar* – originally the title meant a leader of a
tribe but it was later used for a nobleman who
owned land. Between the chapel and the cross
stands a bearded priest.

SCANDINAVIA

E HAVE SEEN EARLIER (PAGES 24–25) how the early peoples – the Vikings – moved out from Scandinavia and invaded and settled far afield.

ENGLAND AND SCANDINAVIA

In the 11th century under King Canute the histories of England and Scandinavia were connected. King Canute of England became king of Denmark in 1016 after his brother Harold died. He then moved into Norway in 1028. This military occupation was followed by Anglo-Saxon priests who converted people to Christianity and built churches.

By the 12th century Denmark had become a power in its own right and later conquered Norway and moved north towards Finland.

SWEDEN

In the 13th century the Scandinavian peoples were not a unified group. In Sweden a number of great nobles ruled the country. Under one of them, Jarl Birger, in the mid-13th century, southern Finland was conquered.

TRADING TOWNS AND THE BALTIC

The Vikings had established a number of trading posts, usually heavily fortified, in the Baltic. By the 12th century trade was in the hands of about 200 German towns which formed together into an association or league called the Hanse (the word meant a fellowship). Trading methods were made more efficient by bookkeeping and buying and selling on credit rather than exchange. The first center for the Hanse was at Wisby, but this was transferred to Lübeck, Germany, in the mid-13th century.

By the 15th century the power of the Hanse declined for three reasons. The Scandinavian countries joined together; the size of the herring shoals in the North Sea were declining; and trade was shifting to the Atlantic coasts.

TRADED GOODS

Foreign agencies were established in England, France, Russia, and Norway. Items of trade included fish, wine (from France and Germany), cattle (from Hungary and Poland), furs (from Russia), metals and wood (from Sweden), butter and cattle (from Denmark), and wool (from England).

Above Detail from a 12th-century tapestry in a church in Skog, a small town north of Stockholm, Sweden. The tapestry depicts the struggle between Christianity and paganism that took place at this time throughout much of Scandinavia.

Left The testing of the sword – a detail of a 12th-century carving from a stave church portal illustrating the story of Sigurd, a hero of Norse mythology. The church is in Hylestad, about 160mi southeast of Bergen, Norway.

Settlements

■ Hanse town (see also pages 78–79)
● Important town

Features located at a settlement

● Monastery
▲ Castle

△ 6926 Mountain peak (feet)
—·—·— Boundary, 12th century (where known)

Feet
6500
3250
650
0

Scale 1 : 7 500 000

0   200 km

0   150 miles

Norwegian
Sea

Lofoten
Islands

Kebnekaise △
6926

Torne

Lule

L Imari

L Olujarvi

Kemi

L Storaven

FINLAND

L Saimaa

Ume

Gulf of Bothnia

L Nasijarvi

Lake
Ladoga

● Trondheim

Ströms Vattudal

● Skog

NORWAY

Glittertind △
8087

Sognefjorden

● Søgne

● Bergen

Lagen

Glama

Ljusan

● Hamar

SWEDEN

Klar

Vyborg ●

● Turku

● Helsinki

Gulf of Finland

Stavanger ●

● Hylestad

● Oslo

● Tonsberg

Vasteras ●

● Uppsala

L Malaren

Birka ● ■ Stockholm ▲

L Vanern

● Skara

● Linkoping

Gotland

Skagerrak

● Kungaly

L Vattern

■ Wisby ▲

● Ålborg

● Varberg

DENMARK

● Viborg

○ Vaxjo

▲ Kalmar

Oland

● Aarhus

● Halsingborg

Baltic
Sea

● Ribe

● Roskilde

● Copenhagen

● Malmö

● Flensburg

● Svendborg

● Schleswig

● Trelleborg

■ Kiel

SØGNE

ALTHOUGH THE FIRST CHRISTIAN KING OF Norway was Håkon "the Good" in the mid-10th century, there had been Christians in Scandinavia long before that. Archeological evidence for Christianity comes from burials and stone monuments in the countryside. Churches must have been built by the missionaries in the 9th and 10th centuries, but no remains have been found so far. Any such churches were almost certainly built of wood.

STAVE CHURCHES

Stave churches – made using wooden planks cut from split logs – were built in Scandinavia to a simple plan. There was usually a rectangular nave and a square chancel with four central posts to hold up the roofs. Some of the churches had aisles. Outside, though, these churches were often very elaborate. Borgund church, shown here, has a series of roofs with complicated and detailed carvings of animals' heads.

Below Borgund church, Søgne, in western Norway, was built in about 1150. The whole church, including the roof tiles, is built of wood. Between 1000 and 1300 all churches in Norway were wooden – about 700 in all. Today only 25 are still standing.

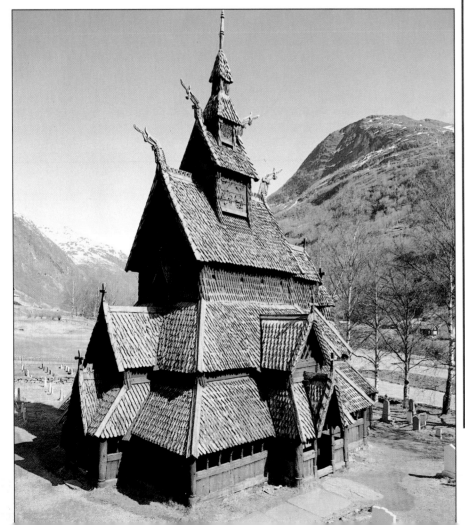

TRELLEBORG

The site of Trelleborg in west Sjaelland, Denmark, is the best-preserved example we have of a Viking fortress. It was built and occupied between the middle of the 10th and the early 11th centuries, one of four very similar circular fortresses. These huge fortresses are unique in western Europe, although some people have suggested that the idea came from two of the Vikings' enemies – the Slavs (of central and eastern Europe) and the Saxons (of Germany).

We know quite a lot about Trelleborg because the site was extensively excavated in the 1930s.

BUILT TO A CAREFUL PLAN

Like the other fortresses, Trelleborg must have been authorized by the king of Denmark. All four fortresses are built to a similar plan. They are round and divided inside into four regular quadrants, marked out by streets that cross the fortresses. The buildings, each of the same type, were set out inside the quadrants in fours around a courtyard. The layout of the fortresses and the buildings is based on a Roman measurement – the foot.

SOLID DEFENSES

Excavations at Trelleborg have shown that the defenses there are of earth with a wooden structure inside. Wooden palisades (fences) held this outer rampart together. At each of the four entrances there were large, heavy timber gates and guard towers. Beyond that was a ditch. Unlike the other fortresses, Trelleborg has another rampart running around it for extra protection.

BARRACKS AND WORKSHOPS

The buildings inside are all made of wood, with the roofs either thatched (as shown here) or covered in wooden tiles (called shingles). They are long, with the posts of the timber frames of the buildings set into the ground. These long buildings must have been barrack blocks for the troops. Excavations also showed that there were a variety of small industrial workshops – such as for metalworking – on the site. It is possible that the taxes collected for the king were stored inside this heavily protected fortress.

Right The fortress at Trelleborg differs from the other three in that it had an annex built (top right). The annex, which is protected by its own double rampart and ditches, contains 13 more buildings of the same type as those inside the fortress.

Below One corner of the fortress at Trelleborg shows the buildings in more detail. The rampart around the outside is built at two levels for strength and to allow access for guards.

Each group of buildings may have had several uses — as barracks, as housing for local people in times of trouble or as centers of royal administration.

GLOSSARY

aisle Part of a church, usually added at the sides of the nave, with its roof supported by columns.

archeologists People who work carefully, like detectives, to uncover the remains of the past, sometimes excavating for evidence, sometimes recording buildings or other structures.

bailey The area of a castle, enclosed by an outer wall, in which the people lived.

barbarians or *barbari* The word used by the Romans for any foreigner living beyond their boundaries who did not speak Latin.

barrow A mound of earth heaped up over a burial.

caliph The title of the ruler of Islam after the prophet Muhammad.

canon A clerk who lived according to holy rules.

castle A strongly fortified place built by the king or a local lord or ruler to protect their lands and to provide a safe place for themselves, their families and retainers.

cathedral The main church of a bishop.

chancel The part of the church where the priest conducts the service.

chapter house The place in a monastery where the daily meetings of the religious community were held.

Cinque Ports The name originally given to five ports on the south coast of England that were granted special privileges in return for certain duties.

clinker-built boats Boats made from overlapping timber planks.

condottieri Mercenary soldiers in 14th- and 15th-century Italy.

crusade A religious war to win back the Holy Lands from non-Christians. The word comes from the habit of sewing crosses on to the soldiers' clothing.

diocese Term originally used for a district of the late Roman Empire. It is later used as a smaller district controlled by a bishop.

Domesday Book A record of property and its owners in England ordered by King William I in 1086 CE.

earthworks A term used by archeologists to describe any remains (of earth) that can be seen on the surface of the ground.

East Roman Empire That part of the Roman Empire centered on the city of Constantinople (also known as Byzantium, now as Istanbul). *See also* West Roman Empire. Also called the Byzantine or Holy Christian Empire.

empire A very large territory, usually covering more than one country, ruled by an emperor.

fief Land granted by the king in return for military service.

flying buttresses Supports of arches built on the outside of cathedrals to carry the enormous weight of the high roofs.

fort or fortress The fortified place for a body of soldiers to live in.

guild An association of merchants or craftsmen.

Hanse A trading association or league of German towns.

hoards Collections of money or valuable goods that were buried or hidden in troubled times but never recovered by their owners.

Islam The religion of the Muslim peoples.

keep The strongest part and last refuge of a castle. It is generally where the lord of the castle and his family lived.

knight Originally meant an attendant. It came to mean a noble who served a king as a soldier on horseback who could provide arms and armor.

manuscript A piece of writing made by hand and not printed.

mercenaries Soldiers paid to fight.

militia Local troops defending Italian towns until the 14th century.

misericords or mercy seats Tip-up seats used by the clergy during long services.

monastic Term used of a cathedral where the priests were monks.

motte The mound, on which the keep usually stood, of the early timber-and-earth castles.

Muslim A believer in the Islamic religion.

nave The part of a church where the congregation stand or sit for the service.

orders Communities of monks or nuns who followed a Rule or code. There were also orders of knights established during the Crusades.

parlement Originally the place for discussion in the French kingdom that became the chief royal court of law.

parliament A group of advisers established by the king in England to advise him. It has never lost the status of the highest court in the land.

pilgrimage A journey (usually long) to visit the shrine of a saint. Pilgrims hoped their sins would be forgiven because they were making these journeys.

shrine A holy place, perhaps where the remains of a saint are kept.

West Roman Empire That part of the Roman Empire centered on Rome (*see also* East Roman Empire). It eventually became broken up into the Frankish Empire and several barbarian states.

FURTHER READING

Reference books about the medieval period

Maggie Black, *Food and Cooking in Medieval Britain: History and Recipes* (English Heritage), 1985.

Mike Corbishley, *Timelink: The Medieval World* (Hamlyn), 1992.

Giovanni Caselli, *A Medieval Monk* (Peter Bedrick Books), 1986.

Giovanni Caselli, *A Viking Settler* (Peter Bedrick Books), 1986.

Brian Davison, *The Observer's Book of Castles* (Warne), 1979.

A. Firth, *Internet-linked Books of Discovery: Knights* (Usborne) 2002.

Kathryn Hinds, *Life in the Middle Ages series: The City, The Castle, The Countryside, The Church* (Benchmark Books), 2000.

Andrew Langley, *DK Eyewitness Guides: Medieval Life* (Dorling Kindersley), 1996.

David Macaulay, *Castle* (Houghton Mifflin), 1977.

David Macaulay, *Cathedral: the Story of its Construction* (Houghton Mifflin), 1973.

John Matthews, *Warriors of Christendom* (Firebird Books), 1990.

Anne Millard, *How People Lived* (Silver Burdett), 1989.

Gwyneth Morgan, *Life in a Medieval Village* (Lerner Publications), 1982.

Don Nardo, *The Middle Ages* (Lucent Books), 2002.

David Nicolle, *See Through History: Medieval Knights* (Heinemann Library), 1997.

L. Sims, *Usborne Internet-linked Book of Castles* (Usborne), 2002.

G Squire & P Baynes, *The Observer's Book of European Costume* (Warne), 1975.

Brian Williams, *See Through History: Forts and Castles* (Heinemann Library), 1994.

Stories about medieval people

Peter Dickinson, *The Dancing Bear* (Dell Publications), 1988.

Cynthia Hartnett, *The Load of Unicorn* (Methuen), 1969.

Cynthia Hartnett, *The Woolpack* (Methuen), 1951.

Rosemary Sutcliff, *Dawn Wind* (Puffin), 1982.

Rosemary Sutcliff, *Dragon Slayer: The Story of Beowulf* (Penguin), 1976.

Henry Treece, *The Road to Miklagard* (S. G. Phillips), 1957.

Reference books for adults

Geoffrey Chaucer, *The Canterbury Tales*, tr. Nevill Coghill (Penguin), 1951.

George Holmes (ed.), *The Oxford Illustrated History of Medieval Europe* (Oxford University Press), 2001.

Donald Matthew, *Atlas of Medieval Europe* (Facts On File), 1983.

David Wright (tr.), *Beowulf* (Penguin), 1957.

GAZETTEER

The gazetteer lists places and features, such as islands or rivers, found on the maps. Each has a separate entry including a page and grid reference number. For example: Alcala 73 C3

All features are shown in italic type. For example:
Andros, i. 83 B1

A letter after the feature describes the kind of feature:
i. island; *mt.* mountain;
mts. mountains; *r.* river

Åarhus 89 B2
Aberdeen 67 C4
Abernethy 67 C4
Adrianople 83 B2
Agal 73 C2
Agen 55 C2
Agrigento 61 D1
Aisne, r. 55 C4
Aix 79 B2
Aix 79 B5
Ajaccio 61 B3
Akkerman 83 C3
Albarracin 73 D3
Albi 55 C1
Ålborg 89 B2
Alcacer do Sal 72 B2
Alcalá 73 C3
Alcalá de Guadaira 73 C1
Alcántara 72 B2
Alcázar de San Juan 73 C2
Alcobaça 72 A2
Algiers 8 C1
Alicante 73 D2
Allier, r. 8 C2, 55 C2
Almeria 73 D1
Alnwick 67 C3
Alpirsbach 79 B4
Alps, mts. 9 C2, 61 B6, 79 B3
Alquézar 73 E4
Amboise 55 C3
Amiens 78 A4
Amsterdam 8 C3
Ancona 61 D4
Andínitsa 83 B1
Andros, i. 83 B1
Angers 55 B3
Angoulême 55 C2
Ankara 9 F2
Antwerp 79 A5
Aosta 61 B5, 79 B3
Apennines, mts. 9 D2, 61 D4, 79 C2
Appleby 67 C3
Ardfert 67 A2
Arezzo 61 C4
Argos 83 B1
Arlaniza 73 C4
Arles 79 A2
Armagh 67 B3
Armenis 83 B3
Arno, r. 61 C4, 79 C2
Arques 55 C4
Arras 55 C5
Arundel 67 C1
Ascoli 61 D4
Assaroe 67 A3
Asti 61 B5
Astorga 72 B4
Athens 9 E1, 83 B1
Athlone 67 B2
Auch 55 C1
Augsburg 79 C4
Aurillac 55 C2
Autun 55 D3

Auxerre 78 A4
Aviero 72 B3
Avila 73 C3
Axios, r. 9 C2
Ayr 67 B3

Badajoz 72 B2
Baeza 73 C2
Balearic Islands 8 C1, 73 E2
Balkan Mts 9 E2, 83 B2
Banff 67 C4
Baños de la Encina 73 C2
Bar 79 A2
Bar 83 B4
Barcelona 73 E3
Basle 79 B4
Bayonne 55 B1
Bazas 55 B2
Beaulieu 55 C3
Beaumaris 67 B2
Beaune 79 A3
Beauvais 55 C4
Bedford 67 C2
Beirut 9 F1
Beja 72 B2
Belém 72 A2
Belgrade 9 E2, 83 B2
Belluno 61 D3
Benevento 61 D3
Bere 67 B2
Bergen 89 A3
Berlin 9 D3
Berne 8 C2, 79 B3
Berwick 67 C3
Besalú 73 E4
Besançon 79 B3
Birka 89 B2
Bjelgorod 85 C2
Blagoveschenskii 85 C3
Blanc, Mont 8 C2, 61 B5, 79 B3
Bologna 61 C5
Bonn 8 C3
Bordeaux 55 B2
Bornholm, i. 9 D3
Borovich 85 C3
Boulogne 78 A5
Bourges 55 C3
Boyle 67 A2
Braganca 72 B3
Brandenburg 79 C5
Braslav 85 B3
Bratislava 83 A3
Bremen 79 B6
Brescia 61 C5
Breslau 79 D5, 83 A4
Brest 85 B2
Bridgnorth 67 C2
Brixen 79 C3
Brive-la-Gaillarde 55 C2
Bruges 55 C5
Brünn 79 D4
Brussels 8 C3, 79 A5
Bucharest 9 E2, 83 B2
Buchau 79 B4
Budapest 9 D2
Budweis 79 C4, 83 A3
Bug, r. 85 B1
Burgas 83 B2
Burgos 73 C4
Bursa 83 B2
Bury St Edmunds 67 D2

Cadiz 72 B1
Caen 55 B4
Caernarvon 67 B2
Cagliari 61 C2
Cahors 55 C2
Calahorra 73 D4
Cambrai 79 A5

Cambrian Mts 67 C2
Cambridge 67 C2
Candia 83 B1
Cantabrian Mts 8 B2, 73 C4
Canterbury 67 D1
Capo d'Istria 61 D5
Carcassonne 55 C1
Carlisle 67 C3
Carpathian Mts 9 E2, 83 B3
Carrickfergus 67 B3
Cartagena 73 D1
Caspe 73 D3
Castel del Monte 61 E3
Castelo Branco 72 B2
Castilion 55 B2
Castledermot 67 B2
Catania 61 E1
Cattaro 61 F4
Cerigo, i. 83 B1
Celanova 72 B4
Châlons 55 D4
Channel Islands 8 B2
Charlieu 55 D3
Charroux 55 C3
Chartres 55 C4
Château Gaillard 55 C4
Chernigov 85 C2
Chester 67 C2
Chieti 61 D4
Chinchilla 73 D2
Chinon 55 C3
Chioggia 61 D5
Chios, i. 83 B1
Chur 79 B3
Citeaux 55 D3
Ciudad Real 73 C2
Ciudad Rodrigo 72 B3
Ciudadela 73 E2
Clairvaux 55 D4
Clermont-Ferrand 55 C2
Clitheroe 67 C2
Clonmel 67 B2
Cluj 83 B3
Cluny 55 D3
Coca 73 C3
Coimbra 72 B3
Colchester 67 D1
Cologne 79 B5
Como 61 C5, 79 B3
Compludo 72 B4
Constance 79 B4
Constantinople 83 B2
Conway 67 C2
Copenhagen 9 C3, 89 B2
Corbie 55 C4
Córdoba 73 C1
Corfe 67 C1
Corfu 83 A1
Corfu, i. 83 A1
Coria 72 B2
Cork 67 A1
Corsica, i. 9 C2, 61 C4
Corunna 72 B4
Cosenza 61 E2
Coutances 55 B4
Covadonga 73 C4
Crema 61 C5
Crete, i. 9 E1, 83 B1
Csanad 83 B3
Cuenca 73 D3

Dankov 85 C2
Danube, r. 9 E2, 79 D4, 83 B3
Dax 55 B1
Demirkazik, mt. 9 F1
Deventer 79 B5
Devizes 67 C1
Dijon 55 D3
Dinaric Alps, mts. 9 D2, 83 A2
Disentis 79 B3

Djakovo 83 A3
Dnieper, r. 9 F2, 85 C1
Dniester, r. 9 E2, 83 B3, 85 B1
Dolomites, mts. 9 D2, 79 C3
Don, r. 9 G2
Dordogne, r. 55 C2
Dortmund 79 B5
Dover 67 D1
Drava, r. 9 D2, 79 C3, 83 A3
Drina, r. 9 02
Dubica 83 A3
Dublin 8 B3, 67 B2
Dubrovnik 83 A2
Dumio 72 B3
Dunaverty 67 C3
Dundalk 67 B2
Dunskeath 67 B4
Dunvegan 67 B4
Durazzo 83 A2
Durham 67 C3
Dvina, r. 9 E3, 85 C3
Dynevor 67 C1

Ebro, r. 8 B2, 73 C4
Edinburgh 67 C3
Eger 83 A4
Eger 83 B3
Eileen Donan 67 B4
Elbe, r. 9 D3, 79 C6, 83 A4
Erfurt 79 C5
Essen 79 B5
Esztergom 83 A3
Etampes 55 C4
Etna, Mount 9 D1, 61 D1
Euboea, i. 83 B1
Evora 72 B2
Exeter 67 C1

Fécamp 55 C4
Ferapontov 85 C4
Ferrara 61 C5
Fitero 73 D4
Flavigny 55 D3
Flensburg 89 A1
Fleury 55 C3
Florence 61 C4, 79 C2
Focsani 83 B3
Fontevrault 55 B3
Forfar 67 C4
Fossanova 61 D3
Frangocastello 83 B1
Frankfurt 79 B5
Frankfurt 79 C5
Fulda 79 B5

Galich 85 D3
Gallipoli 83 B2
Galway 67 A2
Garonne, r. 8 B2, 55 C2
Geneva 60 B6, 79 B3
Genoa 61 B5, 79 B2
Gerona 73 E3
Ghent 55 C5
Gibraltar 73 C1
Glastonbury 67 C1
Glogow 83 A4
Gloucester 67 C1
Gmünd 79 B4
Gorizia 79 C3
Gorodets 85 D3
Goslar 79 C5
Gotland, i. 9 D3, 89 B2
Granada 73 C1
Greifswald 79 C6
Grodno 85 B2
Groningen 79 B6
Guadalquivir, r. 8 B1, 73 C1
Guadalupe 73 C2
Guarda 72 B3
Gurk 79 C3

Gyulafehervar 83 B3
Gzhatsk 85 C3

Halicz 85 B1
Halsingborg 89 B2
Hamar 89 B3
Hamburg 79 C6
Hanover 79 B5
Hastings 67 D1
Havelberg 79 C6
Heidelburg 79 B4
Helsinki 9 E4, 89 C3
Hereford 67 C2
Herford 79 B5
Hermitage 67 C3
Holywood 67 B3
Huelgas 73 C4
Huelva 72 B1
Huesca 73 D4
Hylestad 89 A2
Hythe 67 D1

Iasi 83 B3
Idra 83 B1
Iglau 83 A3
Inch 67 B3
Ingolstadt 79 C4
Innsbruck 79 C3
Inverey 67 C4
Inverness 67 B4
Iona 67 B4
Ionian Islands 83 B1

Jaén 73 C1
Ják 83 A3
Jura Mts 8 C2, 79 B3

Kalmar 89 B2
Kalocsa 83 A3
Kaluga 85 C2
Kargopol 85 C4
Karies 83 B2
Karistos 83 B1
Kholm 85 C3
Kiel 79 C6, 89 B1
Kiev 85 C2
Kilia 83 B3
Kilkenny 67 B2
Killala 67 A3
Kirov 85 C2
Kirov 85 D3
Kizil Irmak, r. 9 F1
Klatovy 83 A3
Koblenz 79 B5
Königingrätz 79 D5, 83 A4
Kos, i. 83 B1
Krakow 84 A2
Krasnokholmskii 85 C3
Kungaly 89 B2

La Ferte 55 D3
La Couvertoirade 55 C1
La Rochelle 55 B3
Lamego 72 B3
Lancaster 67 C3
Langres 55 D3
Larisa 83 B2
Lausanne 79 B3
Le Mans 55 C3
Le Puy 55 C2
Leipzig 79 C5
Lelesz 83 B3
Lemnos, i. 83 B1
León 73 C4
Lérida 73 E3
Lesbos, i. 83 B1
Lescar 55 B1
Les Clairets 55 C4
Lesina 61 E3
Leyre 73 D4

INDEX